The closer Mom came to the end of her physical existence the more she lived in God's Kingdom and the less she held onto the things of this world.... Followers of Jesus live with one foot in this kingdom and one foot in God's Kingdom, and every day ... we have the choice of how much weight we place on each foot.
— *From Book Foreword: Ned Graham, youngest son of Billy and Ruth Graham.*

Herein are amazingly beautiful vistas of Heaven. The stories came alive for me, affecting me emotionally and spiritually. What a privilege to read about the place where we will live—Heaven. In Part Two of *Heaven Tours*, I learned a great deal about the book of Revelation that I had never known before.
— *Keith F. Oles, Professor Emeritus of Geology, Ph.D.*

If we were told to evacuate because of a dangerous oncoming hurricane, the first things I would pack to take with us would be all my Bibles, and my collection of true testimonies of Heaven. Your Heaven book(s), Rita, are in that category.
— *Karen Grafton, Orlando, FL*

I believe God wants you to read this book.
— *Becky Dawson: Mom, homemaker, Bible Lover, Edmonds, WA.*

Heaven Tours

Astonishing Journeys

RITA BENNETT, M.A.

Bridge-Logos

Alachua, Florida 32615

Bridge-Logos
Alachua, FL 32615 USA

Heaven Tours by Rita Bennett

Library of Congress Catalog Card Number: 2009920673
International Standard Book Number 978-0-88270-597-2

Illustrations by Sally Moser.

G218.316.N.m902.35230

Dedication

I dedicate this book, *Heaven Tours*, to my King Jesus—the
Lord, and His best earthly friend, the Apostle John,
and to my dear friend Sally Moser,
the artist who worked closely with me
on the Heaven illustrations.

Rita Bennett
February 3, 2009
Edmonds, Washington

Contents

PART ONE
BIBLICAL VISIONS OF HEAVEN

PART TWO
JESUS' LATEST WORDS FROM HEAVEN

Acknowledgements

I write this acknowledgement in thanksgiving for the Apostle John who was brave enough to write down the visions of Heaven God gave him before his death in 96 A.D. Finally, John is coming into his own in recognition and unveiling of this book of mystery. He wrote of the past, the present, and the future.

People have puzzled over the *Book of Revelation* for centuries. Some have said John was having hallucinations and he wrote them down. Through lack of knowledge, they discredit one of Jesus' best friends.

I never understood *The Book of the Revelation of Jesus Christ,* until the last decades of my life and I do not mean to say I fully do even now. But I understand it better than ever. The sixty-sixth book of the Bible seems to have been written in a kind of Bible coding that can only be clearly understood at the time God wants it to be revealed.

The more one studies both Old and New Testaments, the more the student will see how it all comes together in this final book of the Bible. Students of biblical Hebrew will have more insight than most. I acknowledge the importance of a Hebrew understanding of the Bible, which I have been privileged to have especially in these last fifteen years. Study of the Hebrew language has been invaluable to me.

I'm thankful for David Stern's contributions through his Bible translations. David Stern names the book *The Revelation of Yeshua the Messiah to Yochanan (John).* (Stern, *Complete*

Jewish Bible, 1998.) It is also called *The Apocalypse* meaning the "unveiling."

"The overall effect of so many Tanakh [O.T.] references and allusions (five hundred) is to anchor every part of the book in the God-inspired words of Israel's Prophets." (Stern, *Jewish New Testament Commentary*, 1996, p.785.)

I'm thankful for *The Edmond's Beacon* and Editor Al Hooper for allowing me to write about Heaven in my bi-monthly Worship column and to publish more expanded versions of the Seven Churches of Revelation here; for Kay Arthur's study, *Interpreting Revelation in the Light of Biblical Prophecy;* and *Prophecy in the News* magazine by J.R. Church and Gary Stearman.

I appreciate Bridge-Logos and Lloyd Hildebrand, Publisher, and Peggy Hildebrand, Acquisitions Editor, for encouraging me to write *Heaven Tours.* My great thanks and appreciation go to new friends and colleagues: editor Hollee Chadwick and Art Director, Elizabeth Nason. I've enjoyed working with this visionary, inspiring, and biblically sound publishing company for over thirty years. I'm thankful also for the late Guy Morrell, former publisher.

Once again, I am thankful to the beloved Apostle John because without his faithfulness to write during his exile in *Patmos*, we would have very little knowledge about what Heaven is like. Without his visionary word pictures, there would be few, if any, of the Heaven illustrations in *Heaven Tours.*

In Gratitude,
Rita Bennett, M.A.
September 30, 2008
Edmonds, Washington 98020
www.EmotionallyFree.org

Foreword

by Rev. Nelson E. Graham, M.A.

It was a dark, drizzly North West autumn evening when I found myself following my wife to the front door of a lady I had never met—and somehow I knew this was my final chance. Final chance at what, you [the reader] may ask, so let me back up several months to the events that led me to this door on this night.

For several months, I had been in a downward spiraling depression. I had visited doctors and they had found no organic base for my depression but had still tried to treat it with medication. Yet, it continued and even intensified. I felt totally cut off from God and began to seriously question His existence.

My Self-Worth Plummeted

At the same time, my feeling of self-worth plummeted to the point that I began to feel that my existence was a burden to everyone I knew, and maybe it would be better for the world if I wasn't in it anymore.

The depression was so deep by this point that I was in an almost complete state of paralysis. I literally stayed in bed for twenty hours a day, only getting up to accomplish basic functions and get minimum sustenance.

I Walked Through Life's Memories

It was during this time alone on my bed that I began to go through the memories of my life. The best way to describe it is a long, dark, wood paneled hallway disappearing into the dark, dusty distance with large doors on either side. Behind each door lays a vivid memory from my past and the farther down the hall the further back in time the memory.

For the sake of brevity and to get to the point of this Foreword, behind several of the doors I ran into incredibly painful, repressed memories of childhood sexual and physical abuse.

My dear, longsuffering, and wise wife Christina (Tina) realized that I needed help immediately and asked me if I would be willing to meet with a lady that might be able to help me. I have always been stubbornly and pride fully self-reliant so it was a surprise to us both when I agreed.

A few days later, I was reluctantly following Tina up to the door of this lady I had never met. I was feeling like I was in a surrealistic dream, the rain was dripping from the gutters, I could hear the ferry horns from the harbor below and then suddenly the door opened and a warmth poured forth from within.

A petite woman with blue eyes whom I felt was seasoned in experience greeted us. She had a radiant smile and a bigger heart, and reached out to hug me. I knew right then and there that I was loved and accepted unconditionally. I felt the presence of Jesus but something else that was a little different—a little exciting and unusual—at least for me! This was a house of healing—the home of Rita Bennett.

Healing from the Inside Out

Over the next couple of months, I spent a lot of time with Rita and some friends she introduced me to. I spent a lot of time in inner healing prayer; where you go back to your painful memories with Jesus and the Holy Spirit and let them help you forgive and let go so you can heal from the inside out.

That "something else" I first experienced when I first entered Rita's home was the Holy Spirit. Having grown up within the traditional Evangelical community my focus had always been on God as Father and Jesus as Savior and mediator but the role of the Holy Spirit was always muted. No longer! God is one—yet three!

The Holy Spirit's Empowerment

It is by the power of the blood of Jesus that we can be saved from our sins but it is the Holy Spirit who empowers us with God's gifts to be His tools on earth! You cannot have one without the other.

During this time of depression and then spiritual healing and restoration, I had been on hiatus from taking care of my mother [Ruth Graham] back in North Carolina. With a renewed relationship with God, His armor firmly in place and an understanding of the Holy Spirit's role in my life, I returned to Montreat, N.C., to continue caring for my mom for two and a half more years until she passed, on June 14, 2007.

Spending these last two years with my mom, we had devotions every evening and spent hours talking about this kingdom (man's/Satan's) and God's kingdom. The closer Mom came to the end of her physical existence, the more she lived in God's kingdom, and the less she held onto the things of this world.

Choosing to Live in God's Kingdom

As I witnessed this, it hit me that where we choose to live is an act of "free will." Followers of Jesus live with one foot in this kingdom and one foot in God's kingdom and every day we wake up we have the choice of how much weight we place on which foot. Our daily goal should be to freely surrender our "free will" to God so that we can live as fully as we can in God's Kingdom!

Now I have never been to hell, although I feel as though I have experienced hell on earth. And I have never had a near death experience nor been to Heaven. But I have experienced a taste of what is to come in Heaven.

A Taste of Heaven

It happened one night when Mom was having difficulty sleeping and the nurse called me to come down and be with her for a while. The fire was crackling in her fireplace and the candles were lit on the mantle. Mom was lying on her side staring at the wall above her desk. I sat down gently beside her.

As the shadows danced about the room, I asked her what she was looking at and she said, "The Cross." (On the wall above her desk was a Cross I made for her when I was a boy and hung over it was a life size crown of thorns.) I asked Mom what she was thinking and she whispered "Guilty." And I said "For what?" She looked up into my eyes with her fading sight and tears in her eyes and simply said "For all He has done for me!"

Being a Conduit for Love

I just looked at her in amazement. With all her pain and suffering, she was truly worshiping! I reached out, stroked her hair, then bent over, and kissed her forehead with my hand still on her head and then all of a sudden it was as if God let me become a conduit between Him and Mother. The absolute, joyous, peaceful, warm, exhilarating, unimaginable, all encompassing love of God for Mom was passing through me and her reciprocal love for God was also passing through me.

I just looked at Mom and asked, "Do you feel that?"

She smiled warmly and said "Yes."

I said, "Mom, God loves you so much!" I didn't want the moment to pass, but it did.

I praise God for the privilege of letting me experience a taste of what Heaven will be like when we are in constant relationship with the Father, Son, and Holy Spirit without any of the encumbrances of this world.

For more of what Heaven is like read on with gusto! Rita has pulled together great material that will help you understand that death is not the end, but the beginning. The beginning of eternity that is really beyond imagination!

Ned Graham
President, East Gates International, China
Youngest son of Billy and Ruth Graham
October 14, 2008

Prelude to Heaven

I'm excited to get into the awesome subject of Heaven, but before we do, I need to briefly explain to you about the original *Heaven Tour* illustrations.

Around 1995 I joined a Bible Study on the Book of Revelation with Kay Arthur's videotape series. She asked us, the students, to draw a picture of each of the 22 books of Revelation, as it would help us remember the contents of the chapters. Though I am creative, I am not a trained artist. I dutifully created pictures as requested, and it soon became a fun activity.

I finally studied my way to the end of the Book of Revelation faithfully doing simple sketches as I went. The 21st and part of the 22nd chapter of the Bible are incredible descriptions of Heaven.

As I meditated on the words, I could envision myself having gone through the famous Eastern Gate in Heaven and standing at the entrance to Heaven. I began to sketch it from this viewpoint. The throne of Heaven, I calculated, was in the very center of Heaven and I knew the River of Life flows from the throne toward the twelve gates. Since the dimensions of Heaven are 1,500 miles square, that means the River would be 750 miles long from the center to this Eastern Gate. This was my first sketch and, I thought, it was the end of my Bible Study. (Elsewhere we see Heaven is more than a "simple" square, but rather the size of an enormous cube that we will look at later.)

In the first few years of my first book on Heaven, *To Heaven and Back*, it amazed me that 200,000 copies had sold. I realized that it would be good to have pictures of Heaven on my web site. My professional artist friend, Sally Moser came to mind, so I called her. She accepted my request to take some of my simple drawings and make them attractive, dimensional, inspiring pictures about Heaven.

Sally is the artist and I am the designer. The Holy Spirit worked through Sally's capable hands, mind, and spirit. New creations came as Sally and I worked together from Oregon to Washington State. Eventually we completed seven pictures of Heaven and it was exciting for us to see these visionary pictures on paper. My publisher and I have split them into ten illustrations in black and white with the ten true inspiring stories, and also seven color illustrations centered in this new book *Heaven Tours*.

When Sally had finished her delightful pen and ink sketches, I then engaged a graphics designer to work with me to colorize them for internet use. It was also fun to sit with Taylor as he added the various colors, for instance, differentiating the twelve kinds of fruit on the twelve trees. In my book, I looked up the biblical colors for the twelve precious stones at the gates, the transparent jasper wall around Heaven, and the circular emerald-like rainbow above the throne of God. That helped as we worked through the pictures together.

I eventually sent the pictures to John, the webmaster for my organization, and named it *Heaven Tour*.

Over the years from 1999 to 2009, thousands of people have taken the internet *Heaven Tour* and many have written to say "thanks." I have only had two negative responses and that is an excellent ratio. Others have asked permission to use the pictures for teaching classes at church, for covers of books, for web sites. I wondered how I could share these treasures and yet keep my intellectual property intact. Bridge-Logos, my publisher of *Heaven Tours,* is putting the pictures, commentary, and my new chapters, in this book format so anyone can have a personal copy.

In an email, Steve of Massachusetts said, "As for your web site on Heaven, it is great! I know I need to have permission to print the pictures, but I was so impressed with the Majestic Throne of God that I printed it for my personal prayer time. I hope it was all right? Again, my sole purpose will be for my personal use. Thanks for your response."

I have had some bemoan that their church had rarely taught about Heaven, or described what it might be like. They were quite amazed about the details on the internet pictures with commentary on my web site. I have selected inspiring email responses from the *Heaven Tour* web site that will be shared from time-to-time in *Heaven Tours* and especially in the concluding pages.

In another example, Cathy of Washington State says, "It's amazing! I was so excited I showed everyone at church and they were astonished to actually picture Heaven. Our pastor is very practical in his teaching. I just could not focus on God's Word even though I read it a lot, but these pictures keep me concentrating on God. It is a real blessing and a miracle. Love, Cathy, 2/29/00."

Individual Experiences of Heaven

In this book, we will see my mother, Loretta Jesse-Reed who died in childbirth but was sent back to her children through the Pearl Gate, and Lou Herivel as he met family and friends for a reunion at the Jasper Wall yet came back for a time. Sally Moser through a *death and return* had a View of a New World, and Grandma Phelps left earth in a Tunnel of Light as her family witnessed it.

There is Liz Glover, athlete, who came back to her hospital bed looking at friends through Heaven's clouds, and Dixie who walked with and played her Celtic lap harp, for a new friend right to the *valley of the shadow*. Sherry Calbom, when nearly murdered, traveled toward Heaven at the speed of light then returned, and Shade O'Driscoll who hand-in-hand walked her sister to the edge of eternity, then dealt with more of her own pain.

There's the atheist caretaker at a cemetery that desperately needed a witness about God and eternity, and Forrest Messenger who during a drug overdose became instantly sober during a challenge by heavenly beings.

The joy of this book is that we will experience a *Touch of Heaven* as we go along. Our world needs more of Heaven's light, love, and peace. As we are changed, we can also become instruments of change in the world around us.

It is Heaven now and Heaven forever, my friend,

Rita Bennett
Edmonds, Washington, 2008

PART ONE

Biblical Visions
of Heaven

CHAPTER ONE

Starting the Journey

Rita Bennett

Heaven is a real eternal place, not only an earthly spiritual experience.

There we will find unconditional love, tangible peace, beauty, total acceptance, history, heavenly music, praise, worship, dancing, friendship, family reunions, fulfillment, amazing light, mountains, rivers, and rainbows. We will experience shining gemstones, wisdom, knowledge, learning, thirst-quenching drinks, delicious fruit in variety, heavenly manna, trust, joy, kindness, health, timelessness, and eternal life. These are for starters.

Heaven is the abode of our one God, known as the Trinity: Father, Son, and Holy Spirit. It is the location where His angels, and the saints who have died, call Home. Heaven is a mystery since we have not talked to or read about anyone who has been there for an extended period of time and then come to earth, other than Jesus Christ.

After He completed His "Operation Rescue" for the human race, Jesus then ascended to His Father in Heaven. While on earth He told us, He would come back to get us and take us to Heaven to be with Him. *"I go to prepare a place for you. And if I go to prepare a place for you, I will come again and receive you to myself; that where I am, there you may be also"* (John 14:2b, 3).

Later we will return together with Him to finish earth's restoration and build His Kingdom on earth.

Why Believe?

Why should I believe Jesus' words are true? Because I have had a personal relationship with Him since I was a child. He speaks to me through prayer, ever-deepening study of His Word, His servants, inner knowing, gifts of the Spirit, dreams, anointing, helping others, and life's circumstances.

During my walk as a person of faith, I've watched Him heal the physically ill, cast out evil spirits, mend the brokenhearted, heal the abused, restore marriages, give people abilities beyond themselves, perform healing miracles, and much, much more. Christ, when on earth and now through us—His people—has done all these things as we follow the instructions He left in His Word and by guidance of the Holy Spirit.

Though I have had several dreams of Jesus, I have never had a vision of Jesus or of angels, though I know people who have. I have, however, talked to quite a number of people who have gone to Heaven, and reported that they've seen and spoken to Jesus Christ during a Near-Death Experience. I've written about some of these in my first book on this subject, *To Heaven and Back*; Dr. Gerard Landry, anesthesiologist, is a wonderful example in Chapter Five.

Two times during my Judeo-Christian faith, I feel, our resurrected Lord Jesus has specifically communicated with me. The first was when I had just come back to Christ as a young woman, age 26, and was filled with the Holy Spirit. Soon after, I prayed for an answer to a perplexing question. A teacher during his lecture had said that people are only animals. Before going to bed that night I prayed, "Lord tell me if I am only an animal!" I woke up in the night with these words, "Since you are made in My image, how could you be an animal?" This one sentence answer settled the question for me. It was simple, yet so profound.

Then in 1996, when I returned home after taking a tour group to Israel, Jesus spoke to me in a dream. He told me of the battles ahead of me but the victory I have through Him. He also spoke to me about being His bride (as in the Bride of Christ) and of our Wedding to come. The fellowship in this dream seemed like a reward for taking twenty-four people to His homeland and for going myself—for the first time.

Those personal experiences were several decades apart so I cannot say such encounters happen to me constantly!

You may ask, "How can you give your life to a person you've never seen, and have only had a few vis-à-vis intimate experiences with?" I can because He came to live in me by the indwelling Holy Spirit when I was a child. Most of the time I hear from Jesus through prayer, His written Word, dreams, or an inner knowing. I'm actually hearing from Him in these ways often. We're always in fellowship; that is, unless I blow it and have to repent to restore our lines of communication.

Jesus has proven His love to me over and over, day after day, year after year. Consequently, I believe what He says about the future is also true. His ways will always be beyond my ways (Isaiah 55:8-11).

Why then should I believe some "Johnny-come-lately" with his newly espoused theories, even though he may have many degrees after his name? I have enough revelation from God's Word to last me for an eternity. The Bible is the most exciting book on earth. It tells me about Heaven, shows me the way to Heaven, and helps me take others with me.

What *Heaven Tours* Is About

In this book, you will hear about the eternal place God has prepared for you. You will read some true stories of those who've gone there for brief times and come back changed. You'll read about those whose loved ones went on a "one way trip" to their heavenly Home. You'll read about some who are still not sure about the way to Heaven or if there is such a place.

Throughout the book, as each chapter opens another segment of the tour, you'll see sketches of Heaven according to the word pictures given in the Bible. They are teaching aids to help you visually understand what God tells us about this very important subject of Heaven. At the end of each chapter will be commentary on that picture to help you understand it better.

I think you will have your own revelations as you read and seek Father God for understanding. Many of us in our churches, synagogues, or mosques, have not been given even a good guess from our leaders about how we may picture Heaven. Leaders may reason that, "After all we won't know the details for sure until we get there. Let's not guess."

I believe there is so much we have been given in the Bible that we need the encouragement of attempting to put into pictures what it teaches. I think you and I need all the help possible to assist us in this process of life's beginning and ending.

People Want to Know

After all, we will not live forever in our present state and the world seems to be getting more hellish every day. The tragedy on nine-eleven in the year 2001 killed about 3,000 souls in one day. Wars and rumors of war with bigger consequences than ever swirl around us from the news media. You know all about it as you hear and view the horrors of war every day.

I say it's time to look up and see what God has prepared for those who love Him. When we get to the City of God it may be different from what we envisioned, but some things will be the same. Won't it be fun to compare? I think God wants us to have the joy of picturing what He has told us about, right now, in this life.

Your elderly parents want to know where they are going. Your little children want to know, "If there is a life after this, what it will be like?" They have questions about what they learn

4

in Sunday school, Sabbath school, or Mosque school. A person trying to decide what to believe, would like for you to know enough to tell, him or her, what may happen after this life.

Heaven Tours will assist you in getting ready. Let us get our focus on eternal verities for a change, and let earth and its woes fade to strangely dim.

Are you ready? Then let's go.

The Gate of Pearl Entrance

CHAPTER TWO

A Heavenly Beginning Shaped My Life

Rita Bennett

My mother, Loretta Jesse-Reed, had a Near-Death Experience while giving birth to me. I was her fourth and last child. Physically, she was quite overweight and not in the best state of health. Ever since I can remember, she'd had a heart condition. Perhaps her heart stopped for a short period at my birth.

Though I obviously had to fight for my own survival, I was born looking like a plump doll with rolls of fat adorning my legs, arms, and waist. My older sister, Georgia, said I was a "beautiful baby."

At birth, I was the biggest baby of Mother's four children, weighing nine pounds, ten ounces. Being a fat baby *(macrosomia)* could also mean that my mother had gestational diabetes during her pregnancy that could have caused birth complications. Gestational diabetes usually goes away after pregnancy, though Mom did eventually have late onset diabetes.

Odd that of all her children I grew up to be the smallest at five feet, three and one-half inches, and weighing 118 pounds.

When and where I was born no doubt impacted my life. I'll share that later. Yet it is *how* I was born that has left a lasting spiritual legacy.

Mother Tells Me Her Experience

During my childhood and youth, occasionally my mother's warm brown eyes would look into my blue ones and she'd gently say, **"When you were born, I went to Heaven to get you."** That could have been considered a simply poetic statement except she believed it was true.

It was a powerful, healing statement—I would come to realize this even more than I did during my childhood. Mother would then describe Heaven to me as she remembered it—glorious streets of gold and shining gates of pearl. It was so beautiful and peaceful that she said, "I did not want to leave." She said further, "God let me know He was sending me back because you children needed me." I never forgot my mother's words.

The ministers at churches I attended in my youth never tried to describe Heaven in any detail, although most said it existed and quoted some related Scriptures. During my teens, a few times I remember Mother mentioning her Heaven experience again. I was by then going through a doubting stage and internally wondered how real it was.

How I wish I had believed her more and questioned her to find out further details. In the '40s and '50s, people who had similar experiences to hers were often not believed by the medical or religious professions.

My Mother Had Five NDE Traits

When conducting research for my previous book, *To Heaven and Back,* (published in 1997) and studying the traits of a Near-Death Experience, I found Mother registered five on a scale from one to ten![1] These traits are: (1) a feeling of being dead, (2) a sense of peace and painlessness, (3) a supernatural experience of having left earth for another dimension (out of body experience or OBE), (4) a reluctance to return, and (5) a decreased fear of death.

10

The five remaining traits are: (6) a tunnel experience, (7) seeing people of light (often relatives and friends), (8) seeing a being of light (often thought to be Jesus or an angel), (9) experiencing a life review, (10) a personality transformation upon return.[2]

This last trait—number ten, a personality transformation upon return—I added from Michael Sabom, M. D.. I wonder if this also fit Mother. I'm not sure of counting this trait but I do know that in Loretta's youth she had become a Spirit-filled Christian. Her whole adult life was centered around her faith and her family. I do not know of a further change that occurred in her life following my birth, other than a renewal of her earlier experience with God.

My mother had an attractive face and gentle voice. She was sweet and kind. Loretta was gracious to people and often fed a poor homeless woman who came to our door. I do not remember hearing her gossip, or say unkind things to others or me.

Handel's Messiah

When my sister, Georgia Reed–Danahy, and I were young adults, we sang Handel's *Messiah* in the Tampa Philharmonic Chorus. When we harmonized in the final *Hallelujah Chorus*, I remember watching our mother cry all the way through it. I looked at her in the audience, curiously wondering why she was so moved. Now when an especially inspired choir sings *The Messiah*, and everyone stands to honor God during the *Hallelujah Chorus*, I often shed tears too.

How I wish I could hold Mother in my arms and tell her that I now understand, but I think she knows. In 1967, my mother, Loretta Jesse-Reed, made a second journey through the Pearl Gate, and this time it was permanent.

What is an NDE?

A Near-Death Experience (NDE) is when a person nearly dies, or dies and comes back (often by resuscitation) having had varying degrees of supernatural experience. The ten traits above describe the basic kinds of experiences that NDE researchers, such as Melvin Morse, M.D. (*Transformed by the Light*, 1992), and others have discovered.

We had never used this NDE term in our home, as it had not yet been coined. It is called "Near"-Death Experience because though a person's heart may have stopped beating from two to five minutes, or perhaps longer, they somehow come back and do not stay dead. I know of exceptions to this such as drowning or a lightning strike that can extend life for longer periods of time.

I asked my brother, Bob, nine years my senior and a retired doctor of dental surgery, for confirmation of Mother's experience. He said he remembered her saying about my birth that she had "gone to another dimension."

While writing my earlier two-part book on Heaven, the first half on accounts of seven Near-Death Experiences and the second half a detailed biblical picture of Heaven itself, I then, for the first time became fully aware that my mother had had an NDE. This was an amazing revelation to me that was clarified during my extensive research for *To Heaven and Back*. If I had never done this research in this life, I probably would never have known the depth of Loretta's experience.

"When you were born, and where you were born, has impacted your life." This was stated in an article I read in 1995. When I, Rita Reed–Bennett, first heard this concept, I wondered about it. I would now add to that equation, "and how you were born also impacts your life."

A Quick Dip into the Past

When I was born, Franklin Delano Roosevelt was President of the United States. His term in office was from 1933 to 1945.

That was one bit of security my family must have felt as he led the USA through difficult times. How reassuring President Roosevelt was with his "fireside chats." World War II was looming on the horizon at this time, and Americans were called to live more frugally. So I was born at a serious time in history and in the days of the Great Depression.

Where was I born? In a hospital in Port Huron, Michigan, then a small town established near Lake Huron. The well-known Great Lakes: Superior, Michigan, Erie, Huron, and Ontario, when viewing them on a map, look something like five large leaves on a plant. This port town is situated directly across from Sarnia, a town in the province of Ontario, Canada. A large bridge links the two countries, United States and Canada.

We lived in Port Huron only until I was two. My parents decided to seek a warmer climate because we four children were ill with colds and flu much of the time. The weather was extreme in Port Huron in the winter due to the icy winds blowing across the Great Lakes.

My father, William Harvey Reed, was raised in Port Huron and had two brothers and two sisters who lived there. Most were involved in the First Presbyterian Church where I was baptized as an infant.

Uncle Bob was an optician, Uncle Scott was the owner of a clothing store, and Dad owned a grocery store. Aunt Jane was married to a farmer and Aunt Bessie to a businessman. When we moved, I missed out on interaction with this large, interesting family. Family communication was seriously hindered after we moved away as we were basically limited to letter-writing or expensive phone calls.

Mother, Loretta Jesse-Reed, also came from a large family of nine and was raised in Stockbridge, in the woods of Northern Michigan where they had a farm. Grandpa Frank Jesse had a beautiful singing voice and played the organ. His talents helped to overcome the effects of his hot temper. It is possible that he was fighting the early onset of diabetes as in the early nineteen hundreds there was no treatment for it. The insulin hormone produced in the pancreas was isolated in 1921-1922 by Dr. Fredrick Banting and three others. This discovery was unfortunately close to the time my grandfather Jesse died in the early 1940s.[3]

Mom left home in her teens to escape the conflicts. She did reconnect with her family later in her young adult life. My main connection with my mother's family of origin is that my middle name, Marie, is from her sister, my aunt Marie Jesse–Ferguson.

Recently my cousin Warren Reed, who was raised in Michigan, sent me a picture of Mother I had never seen before. She looks to be in her 20's sitting with two of her sister's-in-law, Bessie and Jane. In it, Mom has the happiest smile on her face. She looks beautiful. It shows her as a lovely brunette, model height of about five-foot-ten, and a perfect figure. I fell in love with my mother all over again.

One of my treasures is a poem she wrote to my husband, Dennis, and me on her birthday February 26, 1967, the year of her death.

A Gift of Roses

by Loretta Ellen Jesse-Reed

Twelve crimson roses came today
From son and daughter far away.
Each one was perfect as their love for me
A rose so sweet and I can see
the wonderful souls so true
deep inside of you

"A rose is a rose."
A rose with a soul so true
for I have waft the perfume
of the soul of a rose

Tender days have flown too fast
when all the children have gone at last
Each one a chosen profession on life's path
but fond memories I hold dear
When crimson roses in garden path appear
I shall know, dears, that your love is near

Just a "twinkle of an eye" away
My love forever will stay
when I see the Crimson Rose
with the fragrance of the soul
in that perfect day

Not far away but near
my Dears to you I will be
when the sweet Rose of Sharon I see.

This is the only poem I recall mother writing and sending to me, though she possibly had written others. Quoting from the *Song of Songs,* she sees Jesus as the "Rose of Sharon" and the center of her poem. She also creatively calls Him the "fragrant Crimson Rose." Her poem shows her belief that being with God, the Son, will cause her to feel close to us, her family on earth, since we are all in the family of God.

Sharon and the valleys were the most fertile districts of the land of Israel. "Coming after the description of our Lord as our Shepherd and our protection, there is a deep significance in this setting forth of His character and relation to us as Myrrh, Henna-Blossoms, the Rose of Sharon, and Lily of the Valleys."

Author Macilravy continues, "As He is, so must she [the bride of Christ—male and female] be in this world. He would have her conformed to His image, with His every attribute adorning her and with every likeness to Him perfected; with every perfume and beauty manifested upon her and in her life" (Cora Harris Macilravy, 1916, p.102, 105).

I think these words quoted from his book, *Christ and His Bride,* also reflect my mother's viewpoint revealed in her poem.

What a loving example my mother was and is to me, increasingly.

A Heavenly Beginning, Reflection

I now realize I was drawn to write about these supernatural experiences not only to heal myself from the loss of my beloved husband, Dennis, who died in 1991, but I was also drawn to my mother's *Heaven and back experience* at my own life's beginning. Being attached to my mother by the umbilical cord at the time, perhaps I had experienced a touch of Heaven's atmosphere.

Looking at the questions of when, where, and how I was born has merits. Perhaps you'll find it so, as you consider these questions for yourself.

Come with me as we explore this place called Heaven, or *Shaymayim* as it's called in Hebrew, a name that has true significance. I'll tell you more about it as we go along.

The tour begins here as we look at the Gate of Pearl where my mother began her journey the first time. She entered it again at the time of her permanent entry through this awesome doorway into Heaven.

Commentary on Chapter Two's Illustration

The Gate of Pearl Entrance

Rita Bennett

As my mother Loretta revealed about her *Heaven and back experience,* she was awed with the pearl gate that she apparently went through because she did have a look inside at the golden streets. I've noticed in my research that not everyone goes that deep into Heaven and comes back to earth.

Still Mother had a choice about staying in Heaven and she put her children first in her decision to return. For this, I am extremely grateful.

The artist, Sally Moser, chose to give the gate an ancient look in this illustration. The rooftop is pearlized as well as the doorway columns, but she envisions the pearl itself in the center of the actual opening where you and I will walk through.

Scripture does not tell us many details about the Pearl Gates. It simply says, *"The twelve gates were twelve pearls: each individual gate was of one pearl"* (Revelation 21:21, NIV).[4] This verse reminds us that there are twelve Gates of Pearl as there are twelve entrances to the City of God.

In my research, I found that there is only one measurement given in Scripture by which you have to guess if it refers to the height of the wall around Heaven, or its thickness (Revelation 21:17). I reasoned that the height of the pearl door and the wall would need to be similar, so my educated guess would be that the Pearl Gate must measure at least as tall as a one or two story building, perhaps more.

You saw the pearl illustration at the beginning of this chapter: *The Gate of Pearl Entrance.* At times, many people will be coming through twelve of these entrances.

Before we speed off into the next exciting story, let's linger at the Pearl Gate and go a little deeper into why God chose the Gates to be created from pearls.

Biblical Symbols of the Pearl

What does the pearl symbolize in the Bible? Jesus is teaching extensively on the Kingdom of God in Matthew, Chapter Thirteen, when He says, *"Again, the Kingdom of Heaven is like a merchant seeking beautiful pearls, who, when he had found one pearl of great price, went and sold all that he had and bought it"* (verse 45,46). What extreme value the merchant placed on this one pearl!

First Interpretation

There are two main interpretations to this parable. First, man is seeking for satisfaction. After trying many things that do not satisfy, he discovers Christ, the Pearl of great price and sells all he has to follow Him. Countless numbers of true disciples have done just that.

Here the pearl metaphor stands for Jesus. Perhaps you are one who has sold all to follow Him. He is *"the way, the truth, and the life"* (John 14:6).

Second Interpretation

The second interpretation is in two parts.

Part One: God is trying to impress us with the value of winning souls to His Kingdom as the supreme good that we should seek. The fine pearls are souls, and we should make sacrifices to obtain them for the Kingdom. Proverbs says, *"He who wins souls is wise"* (11:30b).

Yes, we are called to be witnesses and when we are filled with the Holy Spirit, the power to do this is made available. *"But you shall receive power, after that the Holy Spirit is come upon you: and you shall be my witnesses ... "* (Acts 1:8a).

Here the pearl metaphor stands for winning souls for God.

18

Part Two is this: Jesus, God's Son, gave His all for you. He came to find you, a pearl of great price for himself. He gave His life willingly, out of total love for our fallen human race. Jesus said, *"No one takes it [my life] from Me, but I lay it down of Myself"* (John 10:18).

Here **you and I** are the pearl metaphor.

This concept of the parable goes best with the meaning of the Pearl Gate that follows.

Gentile Believers Included

The pearl is a unique gem in that it does not come deep from within the earth, as with diamonds or gold, but on earth, it comes from abnormal growth in an oyster. Merla Watson, violinist, songwriter, and for many years a music teacher in Israel, emailed me her newsletter.

In it she says, "Did you ever know that pearls are not 'kosher'? Certain sea animals are considered ritually unfit for use according to Jewish law. In Bible times, Jewish women never would have thought to wear pearls.

"So what is meant by the Pearl Gates in the Bible," queries Merla, "the gates we will pass through to Heaven? Simple! The un-kosher pearls stand for the believing Gentiles. It is through the Plan of Salvation the Gentiles received, that we will all enter into Heaven as the New [or renewed] Covenant people of God."[5]

This commentary of Merla's was exciting for me to read as I had been so impressed with the Jewishness of Heaven's Gate when I wrote *To Heaven and Back* that I had missed this part of the picture. It is endearing to consider how God includes the Gentiles in such an important place as the Pearl doorway into Heaven.

I had discovered earlier how endearing it is too for the Jews—that the names above the twelve doorways into Heaven are the names of the Twelve Tribes of Israel found in the Old Testament Torah and the Book of Revelation. In addition, the names of the twelve Jewish apostles in the New Testament are found at the base of the twelve doors.

Even here at the front Eastern Gate—our Lord is trying to show each one of us, Jewish Believers and Gentile Believers, that we are all of great value and that we need each other.

One Pearl for Each Gate

Each individual gate is one pearl, the form of a circle, which is a perfect symbol of unity and eternity. We were baptized by one Spirit into one body, the Body of Christ, at salvation (1 Corinthians 12:12, 13). There will not be thousands of denominations or religions in Heaven, but only one true Kingdom of God.

It is composed of all who have accepted Jesus Christ (Yeshua) as Messiah and coming King. All Believers are Christ's pearls. Our Savior, having given himself for the pearl of great price, is now preparing it for presentation to himself (Ephesians 5:25-27, 32).[6]

So how can God make a pearl door the height of a building one or two stories tall? Let us ask ourselves, "How did God make the stars, planets, and outer space?" Mind stretching as it seems, it is no problem for the Creator of our universe to create these mysteries. After all, He made you and look how complex and wonderfully made you are! The study of the human DNA today is one of the most amazing scientific discoveries.

Now, believing Gentile, look at yourself in the mirror and say, "I'm part of the twelve pearls of God's entries into Heaven and eternal life. My, I'm shiny today with glowing, pearlized colors of pinks, blues, lavenders, over white. I've never looked so good! I bring a message of the Pearl Door, the way into the Kingdom."

Each believing Jew, look at yourself and say, "I'm a part of the ancient path forged by the Tribes of Israel and also the 12 apostles upon whom the congregation is built.[7] I bring a message of welcome and biblical depth to those who come through the gates."

And everyone, including believing Muslims, Hindus, and Buddhists, I want you to know, God's Son gave His life for you too. Through asking to become one of Jesus Christ's pearls, you also will be joined to His eternal family.

Now fasten your Heavenly seat belt and let's ascend for more of the best of all tours.

CHAPTER THREE

Flight Home to the

Heavenly City

CHAPTER THREE

A Message Delivered Before Dying

Dianne Herival's Story

I met Dianne Hiett–Herivel April 29, 1995, at *Holy Cross Church* in Redmond, Washington. There I was asked to speak at *A Day of Healing and Spirituality*. Though our contact that day was brief, Dianne continued to attend other seminars my organization was presenting and our friendship blossomed.

I soon discovered that Dianne is an extraordinary musician, vocalist, and choir director. Since that time, she has sung and led worship at many annual *Emotionally Free* and *Inner Wholeness Lord's Prayer* seminars given in Edmonds, Washington. With her counseling skills, she also serves as an insightful and capable small group facilitator. Need I say what a boon it was for me to meet Dianne that day?

A few years later, I learned by phone and email of Dianne's pain as she walked through her father's hospitalization and his final journey in October 1998. Here is the story of her beloved father and the surprising message **he left behind.**

Memories of a Faithful Daughter

Lou Glen Hiett, 69-year-old retired agriculturalist and avid gardener, and father of two married daughters, had a major stroke Monday morning, October 5, 1998. He was rushed into his hometown's Cascade Valley Hospital in Arlington,

25

Washington. Wife Margie, petite and trim with short silver grey hair and hazel eyes, and two attractive daughters, Dianne and Lou Ann, kept vigil by his side.

By Monday evening, Lou seemed to be rallying. He is six foot tall with no excess fat, due in part, to his love of hunting, fishing, and gardening. Thick, sandy-colored hair mixed with grey set off his northern European features and sensitive, deep-set, blue eyes. Propped up in bed, he was resting as comfortably as possible, talking coherently with his family, reassuring them.

Relieved, Margie felt free to go to their nearby home to take a shower and have a short rest before returning to the hospital. About an hour later, Lou delivered a message he had kept buried in his soul for fifteen years.

Adjusting his lanky body as he leaned against several pillows, he reached out to take the hands of his daughters, each standing on opposite sides of his bed. He observed them proudly. Dianne, age 44, has short, straight, shiny, brown hair, which frames her intelligent blue eyes, and she stands five feet, three and one-half inches tall. Lou Ann, four years younger, is a slender five feet, five inches tall, with stylish, long blonde hair, again with blue eyes.

The Message

Lou looked at each of his daughters and said, "I'm so glad you're both here."

Clearing his throat somewhat bashfully, their father said, "I want to tell you about an experience I had 15 years ago during my heart bypass surgery. I can remember it just as clearly as if it was yesterday. All of a sudden, I was looking down from the operating room ceiling at the doctors as they were working on me. Then for a time I seemed to be in a place other than the hospital. I was somewhere else," he said quizzically.

"There was a glowing, bright light shining in the place I found myself. Many relatives and friends I had known years before were there to greet me, including my father. We were having a great reunion with much conversation. I was having a good time milling around, talking to everyone."

Then I heard a voice that said, "Lou, you have got to go back now." So I did. Suddenly, I was back in the hospital.

"Sure was odd. I have never told anyone about this experience until now."

Dianne who had been reading about Near-Death Experiences over the past year said gently, "Dad, I think you have had a little taste of Heaven."

His blue eyes responded thoughtfully, "Maybe so …" he said, nodding his head. " Maybe so.… I do want to tell your mother about this. Don't know why I haven't told her before.…"

The devoted daughters visited a while longer, then said, "Good night, Dad," hugging and kissing their father before leaving.

Dianne gave Lou Ann a sisterly hug in the parking lot, and got in her car to drive to her folks' house for the night.

Grateful for 15 Extra Years

Speeding along the highway in her solitude, Dianne thought about her father's message. Though he was baptized a Lutheran at age 39, she had never heard him openly share his faith. Such things were considered personal, and he was shy to talk about them.

At times in the past, Dianne wished her father had felt free to talk about spiritual matters with her. Now he had shared this highly personal event with her. His witness was far beyond her expectations. In fact, it was amazing.

She thought, "Dad seems better tonight, perhaps he'll make a turnaround and recover."

It became a *Prayer of Gratitude:*

Dear Father in Heaven, I have already had a miracle. Thank you for letting me know that Dad has already gone to your Home above and then was sent back. I am grateful that You have given him these fifteen extra years with us. I ask You for more time but only You know what is best for Dad. So I ask, as in the Lord's Prayer, "Thy will be done." Hold us in your arms of love at this time, especially if your will is different from mine. In Your Son's name, I pray. Amen.

Dianne pulled her car into the Hiett's Arlington home driveway, familiar to her from teenage years. She drove past several different varieties of apple trees planted many years before by her father. Only a few hardy Jonathan apples still clung to the gnarled old branches. Memories of her children's apple-picking days with their grandpa, and eating delicious apple pies baked by her mother, flooded her meditations. Dianne let herself into the house to prepare for bed, as her mother had already left for the hospital.

The Big One

Early the next morning, October 6, Dianne headed back to the Cascade Valley Hospital to fill in for her mother. She quietly entered her father's room, and sighed, settling down in a nearby chair. He slept peacefully, with a light gentle breathing. She waited beside his bed and prayed.

Dianne said, "Hours passed, and then at 7 A.M., Mom arrived again. Dad was awake and quite lucid, glad to see Mom. He was even wondering if his recent physical problem could have been some kind of food poisoning. He recalled what he had eaten, trying to figure it out.

"The doctor examined him and said 'Lou seems stable, maybe even better. He is, however, still having symptoms of dizziness. My advice is to 'wait and watch,' he said gently."

Dianne describes what happened next, "Mother, my nephew, Joel, and I left for a coffee break leaving my sister Lou Ann with Dad. Returning some minutes later, we were catapulted into a medical crisis, as right there before our eyes, Dad had a second major stroke.

"I knew I would need healing prayer around this memory as we saw Dad look so frantic and helpless. He tried with all his might to communicate with us one last time. But he was slipping away from us. We were helpless to do anything about it. Dad's speech at first was somewhat intelligible, then garbled, then totally unintelligible. We gasped in fear and prayer as he simply became unconscious while his body trembled and shook. We could see his face dissolve as his whole brain short-circuited. We felt so helpless.

"The nurses and doctors were in and out of the room. It was a tremendously confusing time. My feelings and my heart told me right away that this was 'the big one' we had dreaded and that we were losing him. Mom, of course, was crying and deeply distraught. I was trying to be attentive to Dad by stroking his hands, attempting to speak comforting words to him. At the same time, I also stayed by Mom's side physically supporting her.

"Unable to help him any longer, I knelt to pray. Finding myself being supernaturally strengthened, I clung to the promises from Scripture that came to mind, repeating aloud:

Nothing can separate us from the love of God in Christ Jesus our Savior ...

I will never leave you nor forsake you, says the Lord ...

God is our refuge and strength, a very present help in time of trouble.

Lou's Witness

"Looking back," Dianne said, "I realized it would have been far worse if Dad had not shared his 'taste of Heaven' with us as he did the night before he died. My mother was encouraged when right away, I had told her of Dad's heavenly experience, but of course, she wished she'd heard it from him herself. Later Mom realized that Dad had probably not wanted to frighten her by talking about his narrow escape with death. Out of love he'd held back from this admission."

As Dianne spoke to family members, and others, she often repeated her father's message of what she now knows was a Near-Death Experience fifteen years previously. Each time this true story was shared, someone was comforted. Even at the funeral, at Our Savior's Lutheran Church, Dianne was strengthened to share her Dad's final message from the pulpit. She told of this place of light, joy and friendship he had visited, and she added, "He has now returned there permanently."

Dianne told me how one of Lou's longtime male friends from his church, a former high school classmate and football buddy, responded to Dianne's message following the funeral. He said, "If Lou said it, we can be **sure** it is true."

"That is the way everyone felt about Lou Hiett," said Dianne. "Dad was a man of few words, but always those of truth and integrity."

Author's Reflection

I was glad to attend the funeral there in Arlington, Washington and to hear Dianne's dynamic personal witness from the pulpit to a packed church. How fortunate it was that this loving father risked giving his special message to his daughters during his last hours on earth. A healing gift, a treasured legacy, was left behind.

What if Lou had not dared tell his story? We would all be the poorer.

If we, ourselves, have any messages of hope to share, it is important to deliver them ... soon.

Commentary on Chapter Three's Illustration
Flight to the Heavenly City

Rita Bennett

It is hard to get perspective on such a massive place as where Lou Hiett visited once, and then fifteen years later had gone again, this time permanently.

Heaven is called, *The City of God, The Heavenly Jerusalem,* and at least eight other descriptive titles.[8] The illustrations of Heaven given, as well as the others to follow, when in full view are about one-fourth of a pie-shaped slice in the first layer of Heaven.

The full biblical picture reveals that the city is a square, some 1,500 miles on each side. So the blue-green jasper wall is 6,000 miles long. Heaven is 2,250,000 square miles on this level. Later I'll share an even more phenomenal figure on Heaven's size.

Mystery of Heaven's Wall

Sally's picture, drawn for me, is the best picture of the thickness or width of the walls of Heaven. Several Bible commentators and Bible translators believe the wall is seventy-two yards tall. Others, as I do, believe the wall is seventy-two yards thick or wide.

Even though I could not understand why Heaven would need a wall that is nearly as thick as the length of a football field, it made the only sense to me. One of the verses I researched says, " *He* [the angel] *measured its* [the City's] *wall and it was 144 cubits* [72 yards] *thick, by man's measurement, which the angel was using*" (Revelation 21:17, NIV).

This Scripture in Revelation gives only one dimension so a choice of either height or thickness of the wall has to be made by the observer. I'm glad width or thickness was my choice because it led to another discovery about the twelve *Gates of Heaven* that I would not have known otherwise. As you go on viewing the tour, you'll find a most exciting reason why the wall is so thick.

I Chose the Walls Width or Thickness

Since I chose width, the height is still unknown to me except as I shared with you in Chapter Two; I would guess it to be about the size of a large building several stories high.

In this picture, we see a committee of angels gathered around the gate to welcome weary travelers. Maybe one or more had assisted Lou in his trip from earth to Heaven.

Lou Hiett was one of those weary travelers and as he said relating to his first trip, had been met by his dad, other relatives, and friends. What a welcoming committee that was, and the second welcoming must have been an even more powerful Homecoming experience than the first.

Jesus is Preparing a Home for Us

In our Illustration, some of the beautiful homes are highlighted to draw your attention to them. These are the artist's guess about some of the awesome places God, the Son, has gone to prepare for those who love Him.

In the Gospel of John, Jesus is recorded as saying to His betrothed bride, *"I go to prepare a place for you. And if I go and prepare a place for you, I will come again, and receive you to Myself; that where I am, there you may be also"* (John 14:2b, 3).

When I saw in my study of the Book of Revelation that it mentions mountains in Heaven, I was very happy (Revelation 21:10). I love mountains and have the joy of looking out of my living room window, and on a clear day in the winter, seeing the blue, grey, mauve, snow-capped Olympic Mountains.

Some Bible commentators think that the Throne of Heaven is built on top of a mountain. That would be hard to depict if it were much of a mountain so we have chosen to put the mountains in the background. There are some details that you and I will not know until we are there in person.

In the Old City of Jerusalem in Israel, Mount Moriah, Mount Zion, and the Mount of Olives are three important mountains. If you have been to Israel, you will know that these mountains, Mt. Moriah (where Solomon's Temple was built and now where the Dome of the Rock stands) and Mt. Zion (where the Pentecost Upper Room has been rebuilt) are not very tall.

The Mount of Olives is tallest of the three being 872 meters or approximately 2,616 feet tall.[9] These mountains have been eroded through the years and especially through massive destruction by numerous invaders taking over the Holy City through the centuries.

So the Throne of God could be on a mountain certainly not as high as our earthly northwest Mount Rainier of 14,411 feet elevation, for example.[10] It is probably a smaller kind of mountain such as the present Mount of Olives. Following the earthly Temple and Jerusalem (which is a microcosm of the heavenly), it may be on some kind of mountain.

A Heavenly Rainbow

A Circular Rainbow like a glory covering is established over the Throne of God. It has an appearance of an emerald (Revelation 4:3). I love rainbows but this one is different from the ones we have on earth. Our rainbows are in a semi-circle, and they have a full spectrum of colors in them. Heaven's rainbow is a soothing emerald green color, and it is a complete circle, speaking to us of eternity that we have now entered in.

When we see a rainbow in Heaven, it will remind us of God's promise to humankind on the earth. Through it God let us know that after His judgment of gross evil through the flood He put a rainbow in the sky as a covenant with us. It was His first covenant with man. *"And God said to Noah, 'This is the sign of the covenant which I have established between Me*

33

and all flesh that is on the earth'" (Genesis 9:17). Its message is that He will never again send forty days and nights of heavy rainfall on the earth.

I think the fact that God asked Noah to build an ark, and in doing so, to warn the people of that day to get on board and be saved, will remind of us of God's longsuffering and grace. "Noah spent more than a year on the ark" (Hayford, *Spirit-Filled Life Bible,* 1991, p.16). The Bible tells us also that the ark landed on the mountains of Ararat. Only Noah, his family, and the animals on board were saved.

Jesus says, *"But as the days of Noah were, so shall also the coming of the Son of man be"* (Matthew 24:37). Scholars believe that Jesus here is warning us about being ready for His coming. Our Lord is also authenticating belief in the biblical story of Noah.

As we go along on the tour, I'll talk with you about the River of God, Streets of Gold, and Throne of God, and more. This is a preview of the Trip of a Lifetime. The "Home prepared" is available for all who love God and have, or will, answer to His call.

Arrival at the Eastern Gate

CHAPTER FOUR

View Into a New World

Sally Moser's Story

S ally Moser is a petite five feet, two inches tall, eyes of brown, vivacious, and intelligent woman. She is the kind of person you feel comfortable with right away and enjoy talking to.

We met in 1976 when she visited Saint Luke's Episcopal Church in Seattle where my late husband, Dennis Bennett, was the Rector. Later that year she came to work at the church as Parish Administrator. Dennis's *Morning Watch* Newsletter was born at that time. Sally's artistic touch graced the pages of the publication.

Presently, Sally lives in Baker City, Oregon.

Because of her background as an illustrator, I contacted Sally to do the pen and ink sketches for my web site, and now used in this book *Heaven Tours.*

Close Encounter with Death

Part of Sally Jean's childhood with her parents, Claude and Alice Touchette, was spent in a rustic area northeast of Seattle known as Canyon Park. She had one sibling, a brother, Bill, who was nine years younger. When she was three, her dad cleared the land, designed, and built their barns and white shingled ranch house. The small farm had a horse, pigs, milk cow, chickens, ducks, garden, and orchard.

Claude Touchette was a "gentleman farmer," who also for a time attended night classes at the University of Washington, and worked as an electrical engineer weekdays. During those early years, they lived without electricity and her mother cooked on a wood stove; their raspberry patch was shared with bears, and the newspaper was delivered on horseback!

Sally Jean was small and sickly in her childhood due to several bouts with pneumonia, pleurisy, and chronic appendicitis. Rheumatic heart disease and brittle-bone syndrome were additional battles for young Sally. Her mother's favorite remedy was blackstrap molasses to be endured with the same enthusiasm as the morning ritual of French braids, which Sally said was a painful process but kept her unruly blond hair out of her eyes. The family attended Catholic Church each Sunday.

Her parents encouraged her early interest in drawing by giving Sally Jean her first oil paints when only seven years old. Favorite subjects were people and horses copied from Lone Ranger Comic books! She says, "I cannot remember a time when I didn't draw."

At times, she would peel the soft creamy colored lichen off the trees and etch a miniature landscape with a tiny stick as a gift for a houseguest from the "city."

Sally Jean's Story of Drowning

The first two years of my life summers were spent with my paternal grandparents, "Baba" (Bill) and Grammy Isabelle Touschette, in Whitefish, Montana's Rocky Mountains near the west entrance to Glacier Park. During the summers, my light olive skin was tanned from the sun at the nearby lake. I only "played" in the water, as swimming left me out of breath.

Every few days when Baba, a railroad conductor, was in town my grandparents and I—plus one or two of my friends—would stay at their cabin on two acres of picturesque Whitefish Lake. I fondly remember days paddling around on our inner tubes and evenings on the porch eating popcorn and sipping ice tea. My grandparents would watch and laugh or applaud as my friends and I would have contests standing on our heads, or seeing who could walk farthest on Dad's old "stilts."

Grammy Isabelle, who had come from Nebraska on the Oregon Trail, was quite a dynamo and robust swimmer. Each morning, to my slight embarrassment, she put on her navy blue wool, long-legged bathing suit, jumped in the lake and swam to the middle, rested on her back for fifteen to twenty minutes, and swam back before preparing breakfast! Glacier runoff fed the lake so it was very cold and only enjoyed by stalwart locals. The tourists took brief dips.

My story took place in 1949 when I was only eleven years old. Because Grammy was so at home in the water, she of course insisted that I take swimming lessons six weeks every summer. This fateful morning the neighbor girl and I were dropped off as usual at the City Beach for our class, with about twenty other students around our age.

The instructor had reminded us this would be an important day—the class would be "graduating" to the deeper water and jumping off the diving board! The floating dock was about fifty or sixty feet long and about nine feet wide, as I recall.

My classmates had all learned the Australian crawl, but because of my heart condition, I could only dog paddle. I was, however, most comfortable swimming leisurely underwater, as it seemed to require less effort, and it was fun to look around.

The lifeguard-instructor encouraged us to jump off one at a time. Each child would swim back to the dock and boost up or be helped up before the next one was allowed to go. The process for each student took about three minutes.

When it was my turn, I was queasy and apprehensive, and just wanted to get it over with quickly. In I went. Then I paddled back and got a hand-up.

Our instructor said to me, "Sally Jean that was good. Let's see you show the class how to jump in." I was delighted that he appreciated my performance so I proudly obeyed him.

When I returned, he again hauled me out and said, "Sally Jean, do it again, that was even better." I later realized that he was probably only trying to encourage and affirm his weakest pupil. It was my third jump into the cold water but this time it would end differently.

Shivering, but happy, I walked out on the diving board and jumped off. This time as the water surrounded me I found that I could barely paddle, and was being carried down by what I learned later was an undertow. I was being pulled and swallowed by the icy water. There in that location was a deep shelf and drop off from which currents and undertows were created.

Opening my eyes, I anxiously tried to see where I was. I tried to follow the pattern of the boards of the long dock but I could not find my way out from beneath the dock. I had never been brave enough to swim under the floating dock and emerge on the other side like some of my friends. Now out of air, I could not figure out the tangle of logs, tires, chains, and bolts.

I was terrified. "I'll never get out of here," flashed through my mind. My lungs were screaming, desperate for air. I could not hold my breath any longer and gasped involuntarily. Sharp pain tore across my lungs as water choked me. But surprisingly the horrible pain was short-lived and went away. I didn't even feel I was under water.

I Was in a Different Place

I found that I was in a dark, brown place. Someone was to the right of me. He was speaking to me without words as we speak here. Soon my life began to play before me like a home movie.

I saw myself at age three. My mother and I had been visiting a friend. The chair where I was sitting had lovely lace doilies on the arms, which were attached by tidy straight pins. I took the shiny pin out of one of the doilies and wove it into my dress. When my mother discovered it later, she marched me back to the neighbor's house to have me personally return it.

The last scene I can recall in my *Life Review* was at age eleven. Late in the spring before my Death and Return

Experience, I walked a mile to visit the children who lived at the farm closest to me. That day the farmer warned us kids,

"Do not visit the cow. Her calf has been taken away and she is mad! Do not go into her pasture!"

It wasn't long before two of the little children slipped under the fence into that pasture. I was horrified to notice this and realized I would have to get them out of there. Soon the Brown Swiss cow with long horns spotted the three of us. There was a huge gnarled cedar stump in the middle of the pasture that we kids were used to playing on. We ran and climbed up on the stump to safety.

Then to my horror I saw that one little girl who was on crutches had not kept up with the two of us and was still in the danger zone. In that moment, I realized I had to rescue her even if it meant that I would lose my own life. I jumped off the stump and ran to her, dragging her to safety on the stump.

Her crutches were dropped in the process but she was safe from the raging cow whose horns were now attacking the stump. We huddled together to overcome our fear. Fortunately, the adults realized what was happening and came to rescue us.

The angelic or Christ figure continued through these and other scenes of my short eleven years. The incidents either showed my sinful behavior such as sassing my mother, or fudging on the truth, or it showed my good behavior and thoughtful ways. I was happy to know that this "mad cow event" was recorded. Being willing to give up my life for another was the hardest thing I had ever done, but now I was glad to see that I was not a coward.

The man was still with me and I felt secure through these memories. He was sorry for the sad memories but he did not condemn me. When the movie was over, I found myself back in the murky brown place. The man was still with me standing at my right side but yet I did not look at him. I remember thinking how funny it was not to have to move my legs to walk, or my mouth to talk.

After this review of my young life, I continued to notice a tiny pinpoint of light that I was constantly being drawn toward. The light grew bigger as my friend and I went toward it. Strangely, there were no streaks of light coming into the tunnel, though the opening grew to about four feet in diameter. The colors of light and of flowers were gorgeous.

I could hear lots of people singing in a way I have never heard before. Or were they singing? It seemed a blend between various kinds of musical instruments and voices—I could hardly tell one from the other. I could also hear the sound of water, like little brooks babbling over rocks.

The bottom of the scene was like green lush meadows with flowers of outrageous colors. In the distance, I could see what I thought were people in the air, perhaps angels, and people moving around on the ground. My experience of dropping into the entrance of this new world was astonishing.

My Return

Then all of a sudden, I felt terrible pain again. I also felt cold, wet, and confused. I would learn that dozens of people were gathered around. People stood over me wringing their hands as they stared down at me lying on the dock.

Men from the fire department were there in their black coats. They had resuscitation equipment (I understood later), which I saw piled up on the dock near me. The two lifeguards on duty were there with me. My grandmother had arrived after receiving a phone call that I was missing.

I later found that I had been under water twenty minutes! People had been searching for me as soon as they realized I had not returned to the dock. They had probably been searching more at the north side of the dock where I had jumped off, than where the ten or twelve foot drop-off was. It took some time before they realized I was lost under the dock. I still do not know who the "hero" was that rescued me.

As I came to, people began to cheer. I could not yet speak as I did a lot of coughing. I was stunned and uncomfortable by coming into this cacophony of voices from such an incredibly, peaceful location.

Someone shouted, "We need to get help for Sally Jean right away!" Discussion followed.

But stalwart Grandma Isabelle would have none of this. She believed that I might never go back into the water after this horrific event. In fact, Grandpa Bill had been frightened during a swimming experience when he was a child and after that, he would never go into the water.

Grammy announced, "She is going in the water now!"

In her effort to cure my possible fear of water and as the crowd watched in horror, Grammy, still in her dress clothes, picked me up in her arms. She walked with me to the end of the dock, then out to the end of the diving board, and dropped my 60-pound body into the water.

Those who watched also prayed as they saw my head go under and then resurface. They must have heaved a sigh of relief as I now, awakened by the glacier water, dog paddled back to the dock. This time I had to be helped out of the water, as I had absolutely no energy to boost myself up onto the floating dock.

The people who had gathered there were not at all happy with Grammy Touschette's seemingly heartless action, but after all I was her grandchild. Their hands were tied.

Grammy then gathered me up into her arms, drove us the two miles to her home, and put me to bed. I was extremely tired, weak, and sore. It felt good in her cozy bed, especially with Grammy's handmade quilt tucked under my chin. She had given me her favorite homemade tonic, which warmed me and helped me fall asleep easily.

Later, as a teen, I did learn to do the sidestroke and so had improved in my swimming ability. Obviously, I had overcome my fear of drowning.

The Effects of My Drowning Experience

What was a mystery to me as a sensitive child was that no one would talk to me or let me talk about my frightening experience. My grandparents' response was, "We will not be talking about that again," or "We do not need to discuss that."

No one told me the details of how the scene looked from an onlooker's viewpoint. Perhaps part of the reason my grandparents were unwilling to share the details with me is that they were afraid my parents would not trust them to let me visit each summer.

On the other hand, most everyone in town knew I had nearly drowned. For weeks afterwards, my friends and neighbors would hug me, or wave and say how happy they were that I was still here. This dichotomy was confusing to my young mind.

When I got home to my parents, they too were not willing to talk about my brush with death. If I tried to retell my experience, they would just "shush" me. I soon learned that this was a taboo subject and I shut it up in my heart.

Interestingly, when I was fifteen my mother had surgery, and she, too, had a similar NDE experience. For the first time we had camaraderie and communication about our other-world-journeys.

Later in my young adult life, I did tell my true story to some of my close friends and began to learn that many other people had had such experiences. This was liberating to me.

And here I am telling my story to you—in this first time of being in print.

Thank you for being an affirming group of friends for me.

Author's Reflection

You may wonder how Sally Jean could have been under the water for twenty minutes and survived. I'll quote excerpts to you from my book *To Heaven and Back* that will help you with some answers.

Sherwin Nuland in *How We Die* says, "When the brain has been starved of oxygen for longer than the critical two to four minutes, its injury becomes irreversible" (Nuland, 1993, p.40.).

Yet Carol Hopkins, nationally registered respiratory therapist and friend, relayed to me the following. "One exception to this would be near-drowning in a cold (not icy) lake where people have survived up to twenty-five minutes." She explains further, "CPR training estimates four to five minutes until death. In a hot climate you have less time, in a cold climate you have more time ..."[11]

It seems Sally Jean made it by just five minutes, as fortunately the water and weather were fairly cold, as Sally said, "from glacier waters." The circumstances were just right for her return to life!

Sally Now

Sally Moser, now an adult in her late sixties, told me recently that following her near-drowning experience she has always felt secure about the afterlife.

This awareness and security was heightened when at the age of nineteen she accepted Jesus Christ as her personal Savior. She also realized "that man" in her Death and Return Experience[12] was the Lord.

For a while, Sally worked for Boeing for one of the Lead Engineers. This is quite a story in itself as she and her boss had an opportunity to be on the maiden flight of a B-52G. But some military "big brass" had unexpectedly arrived that morning and when straws were drawn out of a hat for the flight, Sally and her boss were bumped. They were very disappointed to lose out on this flight, but it saved their lives. You see when the B-52G flew over Geiger Field in Spokane, Washington there was a mid-air crash with a military plane. No one survived.

Sally told me that this second close call with death was probably the reason she joined her landlady, Mrs. Graham, in attending her church each week. She also studied the Bible with her throughout the week. Mrs. Graham helped Sally Touschette in the formation of the early years of her faith.

Sally years later and now a widow, has four daughters, two sons, and twenty-three grandchildren.

When, in 1997, I asked Sally to be the artist for pictures of Heaven, I did not know that she had had an NDE, or as she calls it *Death and Return Experience*. And of course I did not realize I would be writing a second book on Heaven—*Heaven Tours*—and she would be in it.

Is God exciting or what? I love the way He works in our lives when we give Him a chance.

You, too, are giving Him a chance by reading this book. God loves you and is guiding you one-step at a time. He guided you to join us for this chapter, *View into a New World*.

Chapter Four's Commentary
Arrival at the Eastern Gate

Rita Bennett

How great it is to see at the base of the doorway to Heaven, familiar names of the twelve apostles we have become acquainted with through Scripture study on earth. It's like old friends meeting us: Peter, James, John, and Matthew being four of the best known.

Then there's Andrew (the witness), Philip (not the deacon of Acts 6), Nathanael (surnamed Bartholomew), James –the Little, Thaddaeus (surnamed Judas, not Iscariot), Simon–who is zealous, Thomas (a twin, who did eventually believe), and Matthias (who replaced Judas Iscariot). It will be valuable to know more about each of the twelve before we get there.

The Book of Ephesians says, *"Now, therefore, you are no longer strangers and foreigners, but fellow citizens with the saints and members of the household of God, having been built on the foundation of the apostles and prophets, Jesus Christ Himself being the chief cornerstone"* (2:20).

A traveler now looks up to see names of the twelve Tribes of Israel. Jesus was from the Tribe of Judah, which means praise of God. In Chapter Seven, I'll tell you some exciting facts about these names. What a discovery to find that at the door of Heaven, both Old and New Testament heroes of faith are brought together.

Perhaps the most significant of the twelve gates around Heaven's wall is this one on the East side. The pattern God gave Moses for his tent of meeting in the Wilderness had only one entrance on the East side. Moses, Aaron and his sons also camped near the entrance toward the sunrise (see Numbers 3:38). There are three gates on each side of the foursquare City of Heaven so the distance between them if placed equidistant would be 375 miles.

It's fortunate that we will not have to struggle to walk all that distance as walking will be more like floating and effortless. Any of us who have had trouble with injured knees, ankles, hips, or backs will be delighted to find we have no problem getting around these walls of Heaven.

A tall and stately "guarding" angel is there at the gate to greet newcomers, holding a book in his hands, possibly *The Book of Life*. The lush green of the Eden-like entry we've been walking through has already brought us much peace.

The pillars on either side of the doorway are decorated with huge precious and semi-precious stones. Revelation 21:19 says, "The foundations of the city walls were decorated with every kind of precious stone."

Jasper, sapphire, chalcedony, emerald, sardonyx, sardius, chrysolite, beryl, topaz, chrysoprasus (chrysoberyl), jacinth (hyacinth), and amethyst—the colors would be according to the order given: transparent-sparkling blue-green, rich blue, lustrous blue-grey, bright green, orange-red, brilliant red, gold, sea green, lemon yellow with browns, yellow-green with bluish hue, deep red-brown, and luxurious purple. What a glorious array of rainbow colors meet our eyes!

Yes, the visually impaired when on earth, are able to see it completely now. All are awestruck, but they even more so.

There is so much history and beauty to see, we can barely take in even a fraction of it. What we've been praying for and living for is now complete. We are Home, and ready to step over the threshold of the awesome Kingdom of God.

Tunnel of Light into Heaven

Grandma's Journey Into the Light

Winifred Phelps's Story

It was amazing for me to hear about the unique phenomenon that occurred when Winifred Phelps's grandmother died. It happened back in 1935. I learned of this true story from mutual friends, Phyllis Morgan and Betty Bell. They made the initial contact with Winifred for me.

I learned that young Winnie at that time of her history, was nine and a-half years old and lived in Rainier Valley, Seattle, Washington. She had straight, shiny, brunette hair, grey-green eyes, and a fair complexion. Her Aunt Lizzie who lived nearby cut her hair short and gave her bangs. It was a friendly neighborhood with lots of children to play with. Winnie's favorite activity was riding her bike. She also played Hide and Seek and Tag with her friends.

Winnie's Story

My parents Erwin and Myrtle, my twelve-year-old sister Harriet, and I lived with my widowed grandmother, Elizabeth Neil, on Angel Place. She looked rather angelic herself, grey hair piled on top of her head, with a five foot, eleven inch willowy figure.

My maternal Grandma Neil was raised in Glasgow, Scotland, married there and gave birth to six children. After her children were raised and Grandpa Neil died, Grandma came to America. The adult children and their mates followed.

Shortly after her arrival, she was looking for a place to build a home. Grandma walked down a little dirt path in Rainier Valley, Washington and ended up falling in love with this two-block plot of land. She named it right then and there, in her Scottish brogue, "Angel Place." "This" she said, "is wherree I want to spend the rreest of my days."

My dad and Uncle George built her a one-story frame house with four bedrooms, and painted it white with a pale green tint. My family and I lived there with Grandma. The land was parceled off and the other lots were sold, making a nice profit.

Grandma Neil was very religious. She got her six children, including my mother, to consistently attend Presbyterian or Baptist churches. Grandma demanded it not only of her children but also eventually of her fifteen grandchildren. In fact, that's where I got my early religious education. As we gathered around the table to eat, we always had grace before meals.

A Brilliant, Vibrating Light

Years went by and then one blustery September day Grandma Neil became real sick. At this time, she was seventy-seven years old. My folks realized that grandma was not going to live very long so they shared the news with Aunt Lizzie and Uncle George, and Aunt Belle. All three came to the house and joined us overnight.

In the middle of the night while we were all sleeping, a bright light lit up the whole house. It woke up the entire household. The light was brighter than any electric light that I have ever seen. When it lit up the house, we all ran into Grandma,'s room and found that her room was the brightest. It was just extreme. Her bed was all lit up and her body was vibrating with light. We stood there and stared at her for a few minutes. We were scared speechless.

Then there appeared a path of light that ascended upward. It was about a yard wide, and it went from her bed to the corner of the room. Her spiritual being was illuminated with this light. It gradually drifted over to a bunch of light that appeared to be going to the corner of the room. The only way I can explain it is that while her body lay there in bed, her spirit was going up into the light and then out through the ceiling of the room.

The Darkest Dark

Suddenly the house was dark. I mean really dark! We did not have any interior nightlights, or even outdoors streetlights in those days; it was just the darkest dark I have ever known. My mother fainted, and in the darkness, my Uncle George accidentally fell on top of my mother! What a commotion took place.

Realizing what happened, my dad yelled at everybody, "Stand still, and do not walk on Mother!"

Dad could not get to the light switch easily, so he ordered everybody, "Stand still, and do not move."

Slowly he felt his way along the wall until he got into the hall and turned on the hall light. In comparison to the light that had been on her body, the electric light was not very bright at all.

When we finally got all the lights on and revived mother, my Aunt Lizzie went over to the bed, looked at Grandma, and said with finality, "She-is-dead."

But I also knew in my child-heart, "She-is-alive!" After all, I saw her leave.

But then everyone in the room saw this phenomenon, not just me. Everyone in this group of seven: that is, five adults and two children, believed it. Everybody knew it, as we had experienced it together.

Winnie's Reflection

Winifred is now in her mid-70s and a retired businesswoman. Her brunette hair is grey, still short, but with no bangs. She never grew tall like her grandma—her full growth was five feet, four inches. Winnie, as she is still called by close acquaintances, has a sweet smile and is a friendly person. At the age of twenty-one, she served as a missionary to Anchorage, Alaska, for a time. She presently lives in Shoreline, Washington.

I asked Winnie how her experience at her grandma's death changed her life. "Two things happened," she said.

"First, after the *death experience*, my Aunt Belle came to live with us awhile to help in our recovery. Aunt Belle was religious like her mother and around that time, I accepted the faith of my grandma, becoming a believer in Jesus Christ for my salvation. My life was changed forever. I think Grandma's supernatural departure helped me have faith that there is a life after this one.

"Second, it seems I had been prepared for the biggest shock of my young life. Only six months later, in February 1936, my mother died from cancer. She went into the hospital and never came out. Our whole lives were turned upside down. Dad was the most traumatized by Mom's death. I was sent to live with an aunt in Snohomish. My sister, Harriet, went to live with another aunt in Port Townsend. After several years, my father sold the house on Angel Place and our lives were never the same.

"Yet one thing I know is that I have never doubted that God is real. I have since my childhood lived my life as a faithful believer and witness to my Lord's power all these seventy-five years."

Author's Reflection

This true story is not a Death and Return Experience nor a Near-Death Experience, but a *Supernatural Death Experience*. Perhaps Grandma Elizabeth Neil's extraordinary experience was like part of Heaven's Tunnel of Light touching down on earth to assist in her departure. She did not come back to earth but remains to this day on the other side. There she experiences the glorious light of Heaven, called *Shekinah* or glory in the Bible.

Chapter Five's Commentary
Tunnel of Light in Heaven

Rita Bennett

The tunnel of light entrance is an amazing revelation given as the artist, Sally Moser, worked with the dimensions I gave her from Revelation 21:17. I was so excited when she completed the drawing and sent it to me. I sat in amazement as I looked at the completed illustration. I was excited to see how it turned out to definitely be a tunnel of light into Heaven.

This outcome was a surprise to us both. The tunnel lights up so brightly as the reflection from the Throne of God and presence of the Lord glistens through the transparent Jasper wall entrance.

Now we know why God chose to make the wall around Heaven so thick, seventy-two yards thick. He must have wanted each of the twelve entrances to be a tunnel of light! Three tunnels of light are on the north, three tunnels of light on the south, three tunnels of light on the east, and three tunnels of light on the west of Heaven. What a radiant place!

What also thrilled me with this revelation was that many dying people as they go into eternity describe to those by their bedside that they see a tunnel of light. And many people who have died, or nearly "died and come back" (NDEs), describe going through a tunnel.

It was not known until this time that the Bible actually confirms a tunnel of light entrance. To our knowledge, this is a first-time discovery.

I found it necessary to read many books on Near-Death Experiences during my research for *To Heaven and Back*. I soon found some non-theistic authors who explained the tunnel experience simply as the human brain dying from the outside cortex inward, death moving layer by layer until it reaches the core of the brain. This to them explained the tunnel of light experience until, according to their belief system, that person went into oblivion. How could the evolutionary process be so wise as to provide this awesome tunnel experience for the dying and then there be only darkness, lights out forever?

Even some Christian leaders have debated about the authenticity of those who experienced a tunnel of light experience because they did not think it was biblical. I can certainly understand their concern, but here Sally Moser and I present, through Scripture and illustration, evidence for this phenomenon.

How great it is to find that the Angel of God has already proclaimed this truth to the Apostle John two thousand years ago! (Revelation 21:17). This discovery was revealed following the publication of *To Heaven and Back,* and dated by Sally on the original picture first sketch 11/97, then with final edits 8/99, and established on my web site in January 2000. This is the first time of writing about it in a book with the picture available to all in *Heaven Tours.* The recent *Heaven Tours* book cover was inspired by our own illustration, *Tunnel of Light into Heaven,* used with my permission for this book.

Precious Stones at the Gates

Here artist and author chose to place the colorful precious stones at the foundation and bottom of each of the gates. Bible scholars have different opinions about the location of the precious stones. The most familiar stones to us are sapphire (blue), emerald (green), topaz (golden), and amethyst (purple). (See *To Heaven and Back* for more details on the gemstones.)

Drawn to the light of Christ at the end of the transparent Jasper Tunnel of Light, the joyous person in the picture hurries on to the new life ahead. There is no more sadness, sickness, sorrow, fear, or disappointment, and every tear is wiped away, except for tears of joy.

Front Door View of Heaven

CHAPTER SIX

Glorify God in Everything—
Even a Marathon

Liz Glover's Story

In 1994, I met Liz Glover, Ph.D., Physical Education Professor
at the University of Oregon. We connected at a Healing
Work Shop in Eugene, Oregon. Since that time, we have
worked together in leadership at *Emotionally Free Seminars*
in Washington State, Oregon, and Maine.

Liz's healing prayer-ministry almost came to a halt in year
2002. Here is her story.

The Goal: *"I press toward the goal for the prize of the
upward call of God in Christ Jesus"* (Philippians 3:14).

On October 6, 2002, I walked the Portland Marathon in nine
hours and four minutes. That experience was a milestone for me
in my life. Since 1972, I have had the desire to run a marathon.
I had visited Marathon, Greece and observed the monument
depicting Phidippides, the Athenian army messenger, who ran
from Marathon to Athens and died. But of course, now people
run marathons all the time and do not die, and I had the idea
that I could do it too.

The Training: *"Train up a child in the way he should go, And
when he is old he will not depart from it"* (Proverbs 22:6).

By age 53, I had stopped running because of foot problems and arthritic knees, but I was walking. In 2001, I heard about a course called Marathon Walking Training so immediately I signed up and began my training in January of 2002. The training was very intense. We walked seven days a week. One day we did sprints (1 - 3 minute fast walk) up a slight incline and working up to a total of twenty sprints in one hour. Another day we did fast walk for 15, 30, or 45 minutes. And on the weekends we had long walks over mountains and hills for endurance.

It was amazing that even though I had vacations and trips interfering with my training, I was still able to keep up with the class. Near the end of the training, I began to ask myself, "Why am I doing this? What is God's plan for my doing this marathon?" It occurred to me that God could be glorified in marathon walking. I usually walk alone. Most of my walking friends were faster and they talked a lot. I like to maintain a steady pace, get into a steady rhythm, and I think a lot. I even like to pray while I am walking.

The Race*: "Do you not know that those who run in a race all run, but one receives the prize? Run in such a way that you may obtain it"* (I Corinthians 9:24).

On October 5, I drove to Portland, checked into my motel—Days Inn—and prepared for the walk on Sunday. I was up early Sunday morning, dressed and ready to go. As the gun sounded, we were off—many, many runners and walkers for the 26.6 mile experience. After the initial excitement of walking through downtown Portland, I began to think about my purpose in this experience—to glorify God.

So I prayed during my walk: "Put on the whole armor of God" (Ephesians 6:11), The Lord's Prayer, and The Good Shepherd Prayer. It was very uplifting. I also followed the directions given to me in the Race Information: Drink water and/or Gatorade at every station. So at every station, which were two miles apart, I had a cup of water or a cup of Gatorade.

I also visited the "Honey Buckets" at every station, because I was not used to consuming so much liquid. It was NOT a hot day and I was NOT perspiring.

The Finish: *"I have fought the good fight, I have finished the race, and I have kept the faith"* (2 Timothy 4:7).

At approximately 4 P.M., I walked across the finish line and met my coach, Tyler, and she had me eat immediately. I did not feel like eating for I was exhausted. All I wanted to do was to lie down and extend my legs and feet upward and towards my head. Stretching felt good. Even though I was experiencing a little dizziness and buzz, I managed to walk another block to pick up my winner's t-shirt and another four blocks to my motel. When I arrived at the motel at approximately 4:30 p.m., I got sick.

Recovery from the Race: *"Let us lay aside every weight, and the sin which so easily ensnares us, and let us run with endurance the race that is set before us, looking unto Jesus, the author and finisher of our faith"* (Hebrews 12:1-2a).

After resting, I called my friend, Pamella, and we arranged to eat at 6:30 P.M. That gave me two hours to rest, shower, dress, and recover. But I did not recover. I was still dizzy when I went to the lobby at 6:30. I told Pamella and her husband, Bret, that I did not feel good, and I was too tired to eat. I returned to my room, ate fruit, and drank cranberry juice.

Then I called the desk and asked for some saltines. The desk clerk brought them to me, and I went to the door and thanked her. Even after eating the saltines, I did not feel good. So around 7:30, I called the desk and said, "I need a physician." The desk clerk told me to call 911. I sat back on the bed and did NOT call 911.

After awhile I noticed a woman standing in front of me. She was the desk clerk. Then I got sick again. I knew I was in trouble. I had no idea how she entered the room. I was humiliated that I got sick in front of her. I apologized to her, and she said it was okay.

I asked, "Is an ambulance coming?" and she responded, "Yes." Then I experienced Jesus' peace. I felt His presence there in the room with me. I rested in His peace.

Finally, the ambulance attendant came and got my attention by yelling, "What's your name?" Amazingly, I was able to tell him my name even though I was frightened by him and trembling. Immediately, I had a seizure and went into a coma.

Twenty-four Hour Trauma: *"He who dwells in the secret place of the Most High shall abide under the shadow of the Almighty. I will say of the Lord, 'He is my refuge and my fortress; My God, in Him I will trust'"* (Psalm 91:1-2).

I was a Jane Doe. And for this Jane Doe, the ambulance service had the assignment of taking me to Oregon Health Sciences Hospital. Since I was unconscious, I really do not know what took place during those 24 hours. I am relying completely on what people have told me. I was fortunate to be taken to a research hospital, and received the best care.

Approximately 18-20 hours after the start of the coma, I became acutely aware that I needed to go to the bathroom. Nature was calling! I attempted to get up and climb out of the bed. Wires were all over me, and I wrestled with them. The nurses were there, and they tried to calm me and keep me down.

After several attempts, and hearing them say, "No, No, No!" I heard them say, "Okay, let's get her up." What a relief! Even though I was connected to a catheter, it was just great to be sitting for while. I really do not remember anything during that 24-hour period, except this one experience of trying to get out of the bed and the nurse who said, "Okay, let's get her up."

Identifying Jane Doe: *"A good name is to be chosen rather than great riches"* (Proverbs 22:1a).

When I went to the hospital, at about 8:30 that Sunday evening, the ambulance attendant had my wallet, and cell phone. Around 10 p.m., the emergency room doctor called the first number on my cell phone. It was my brother's telephone number in Charlotte, North Carolina and it was one o'clock in the morning there. My sister-in-law, Ann, answered the phone.

The doctor said, "Do you know Elizabeth Glover?" Ann said, "Yes, she's my sister in-law." The doctor told her that I was in a coma, and she immediately gave the phone to my brother, John, who is also a physician. The doctor informed John that I had hyponatremia (water intoxication) and that they were attempting to bring my electrolytes in balance.

But I guess the hospital was hoping that someone, a friend or family member, could come and talk to me, as I was not responding to anyone, even though my eyes were open. The attendants thought I had a stroke.

John and Ann had no information about my doctor or anyone who could be of assistance to me while I was in the hospital. So, in the early hours of morning, Ann began calling all Episcopal churches in the Eugene-Springfield area, and she left messages on their answering machines. She informed every Episcopal Church that I was in the OHSU hospital and in a coma and she hoped that someone would respond to this call.

Ann also called St. Thomas Episcopal Church in Camden, Maine, where Rita Bennett and friends (I was one of them) had that year conducted an *Emotionally Free Seminar*. That church was able to give Ann Rita's telephone number, and Ann called Rita with the hope that prayers might bring me back to life.

Family and Friends Answer God's Call: *"Is anyone among you sick? Let him call for the elders of the church, and let them pray over him, anointing him with oil in the name of the Lord"* (James 5:14).

Ann's telephone calls alerted many friends to pray for me. My priest, Fr. Ted Berktold, called Pamella's mother, a member of my church. Eventually he called Pamella and Pamella was able to leave her job and come to the hospital. The doctors were hoping that I might talk with her. I just looked at her. There was no response on my part and I do not even remember her being there.

Then my friend, Rita Bennett, called and prayed for me over the telephone. Fortunately, the nurse accepted Rita's request to hold the phone to my ear while she prayed. Although I never heard her consciously, I believe Rita's prayers were received by my soul.

Fr. Ted also contacted my good friend, Lois, who has been my teaching colleague for forty years. Although Lois is more interested in sports than church, this incident gave her an opportunity to have a personal dialogue with my priest. And most recently, I understand that the Bishop of Oregon was notified about the incident. So many people were praying for my recovery, and it was very successful.

Recovery from the After-Effects*: "And the prayer of faith will save the sick, and the Lord will raise him up"* (James 5: 15).

Still in a coma, about 8:00 P.M. on Monday night, I heard someone call out, "Liz!" I looked in the distance and there were two people, a man, and a woman. A cloud seemed to surround them, and I thought, "Oh, I think someone is coming for me!" Then, I heard it again, "Liz! It's Pamella."

When I realized that Pamella and Bret were the couple within the cloud, I said, "Hi Pamella." Pamella raised her hand and shook a little pink address book and said, "Liz, what about your cats?" I looked at the clock and it was close to 8:30 P.M. I had no idea how long I had been in the hospital, so I thought about the cat sitters.

Then, I slowly said, "Critter...Critter...Sitter!" It took me a long time to say those words, but at least the doctors and nurses, who were standing by and observing, were aware that I was finally recovering. Before Pamella left that night she gave me my Bible, which I had left in my hotel room. I wasn't sure why she thought I would need it.

The next day Rita phoned me again. She talked with me and told me that she had a Psalm for me. It was Psalm 91: "He who dwells in the secret place of the Most High shall abide under the shadow of the Almighty. I will say of the Lord, 'He is my refuge and my fortress; My God, in Him I will trust.'" She read the entire Psalm to me. And I also read it several times in my room from my own Bible, which Pamella had brought to me.

The recovery took two more days with all kinds of tests on my neurological system. Finally, Bret drove me home in my car on Wednesday afternoon, and Pamella came in her car and took him back to Portland. What wonderful friends I had in the hospital, in Portland, in Eugene, in Seattle, and in Charlotte!

Giving Thanks to God: *"Praise the Lord! Praise God in His sanctuary; Praise Him in His mighty firmament! Praise Him for His mighty acts; Let everything that has breath praise the Lord"* (Psalm 150:1, 2, 6).

I had an opportunity to tell Fr. Ted about the experience, particularly the one of coming to and seeing Pamella and Bret "in a cloud." Was I close to Heaven? Were these people in Heaven possibly friends greeting me? No, they were friends on Earth greeting me!

Fr. Ted's response was, "Liz, God did not want you to die!"

I am so thankful to be alive! I served in church that next Sunday, one week after the race. I was a Lay Eucharistic Minister and I said the prayers for the people. One of the prayers I was to pray was for myself, "Let us give thanks for the recovery of Liz Glover."

It seemed miraculous that I could be glorifying God in a marathon on one Sunday and giving thanks to God for my life on the next Sunday.

In everything, let us glorify the Lord, giving Him praise and thanksgiving. Amen.

Author's Reflection

Liz asks a question about the cloud she saw her friends through, "Was I close to Heaven?"

One wonders just how a cloud can get into a hospital room. Being in a coma for twenty-four hours does seem to be getting closer to Heaven! Let's look at a few verses about clouds in the Bible.

When Jesus' work was finished on earth, He said these final words: *"But you shall receive power when the Holy Spirit has come upon you; and you shall be witnesses to Me in Jerusalem, and in Judea and Samaria, and to the end of the earth"* (Acts 1:8). These are dynamic powerful words Jesus gave to His disciples, and they are also given to us today.

"Now when He had spoken these things, while they watched, He was taken up, and a cloud received Him out of their sight."

Luke, the writer of Acts speaks of Christ's Ascension, *"And while they looked steadfastly toward Heaven as He went up, behold, two men stood by them in white apparel, who also said, "Men of Galilee, why do you stand gazing up into Heaven? This same Jesus, who was taken up from you into Heaven, will so come in like manner as you saw Him go into Heaven"* (Acts 1:9 – 11).

Here the Angel says Christ left in the clouds and will return in the clouds. It seems that wherever clouds are mentioned in the Bible they are usually connected with God.

"So Moses went into the midst of the cloud and went up into the mountain. And Moses was on the mountain forty days and forty nights" (Exodus 24:18). The Children of Israel

experienced the miracle of a cloud covering in the wilderness daily for forty years.

Nahum says, *"The clouds are the dust of His feet"* (1:3).

There are natural clouds and supernatural clouds. I think Liz experienced supernatural clouds as a sign from God. Wherever she went during her 24-hour coma, she came back in a cloud of glory.

Chapter Six's Commentary
Front Door View of Heaven

Rita Bennett

Though I'm not an artist, I did not know that my first simple effort of drawing a picture of Heaven would be the beginning of a little bit of Heaven on earth. The very rough picture I called a "Front Door View of Heaven" in the front of this chapter came through an exercise in my research as I studied the Book of Revelation for several years and attempted to draw a picture of each of the 22 chapters.

The initial purpose of my simple pictures was to look at them as aids in remembering everything in each chapter. When I got to chapter twenty-one, I was amazed that the first thing the traveler from earth to Heaven sees as he or she walks into Heaven's entrance is an amazing boulevard.

In Sally Moser's lovely rendition of the "Front door of Heaven," immediately one sees a flowing river of life, and on each side of the river is a kind of Garden of Eden graced by six Trees of Life one each side for a total of 12 trees with 12 kinds of fruit on each tree. Then flanked on either side of this sight are the amazing 750-mile long streets of gold.

Liz Glover was very close to running a personal marathon down one of these streets of gold. I'm very glad that it was not time for Liz to finish her heavenly race on these pure transparent gold streets!

Now that would be a real marathon for all of us to plan on running one of these days. Don't worry, 750 miles will be easy in our new heavenly bodies.

The City Foursquare

Heaven is called by many descriptive names. One is "The City Foursquare" because it is a square of 1,500 miles on each side (total length of the wall around the City is 6,000 miles). Since the Throne of God is in the middle, the River of Life would also be 750 miles long. The river issues from under the Throne, perhaps flowing toward all twelve gates the same as with this primary one on the East.

Here is another place in this description where we see similarities of the New Jerusalem and Old Jerusalem. Many Believers are looking forward to the Millennial Reign of Messiah when He returns to earth. At that time, it is believed that rivers of water will issue from the Throne of the rebuilt Temple in Jerusalem.

Rebecca Springer in her book tells of her vision of Heaven at a time when she nearly died. (Springer, *Within the Gates,* 1995.) During four days in a coma, she said she experienced bathing in the River of Life as a cleansing, refreshing, and healing experience. That is a personal testimony and wonderful to think about.

With such incredible fruit on the trees at the entrance, undoubtedly it is there to be enjoyed. It will be the experience of a lifetime, eating fruit that satisfies our entire being and fulfills our eternal life.

One mother, Lauren, wrote to me on the internet saying, "My five year old son is always pestering me with questions about Heaven—'Where is it? What does it look like?'—as only a five year-old can. Now I can finally show my son just a hint of what we have to look forward to some day. It was so wonderful!

"He really got excited and said he couldn't wait to get there. He wanted to know if we could eat the fruit of the trees and if it would taste good! Thanks so much for doing the work to put this web site together. I know God is in it." (Year 2000.)

If you could zoom in by computer, you would get a better look at the people walking toward the Throne praising God, arms lifted in praise. What a happy scene!

That can be us someday. He has prepared great things for you. Take time to relax right now, take a deep breath, and speak praises to God. Rejoice!

A Coded Message
for you over
the Gates of Heaven

Judah: Confessors and praisers of God,

Reuben: Looking upon the Son,

Gad: A band of,

Asher: Blessed ones,

Naphtali: Wrestling is over,

Manasseh: Forgetting the pain,

Simeon: Hearing and obeying His Word,

Levi: Cleaving to our Lord,

Issacahr: Who is our reward,

Zebulun: We are home,

Joseph: We are added to the family of Jesus,

Benjamin: Son of the Father's right hand

Coded Message on the Gate

CHAPTER SEVEN

Through the Valley

Dixie Nash's Story with Joan Husby

Dixie Nash is a Lutheran minister, wife, mother, and harpist. I met her at a beginning Hebrew Language Course. We had a lot in common and she visited my home a number of times, meeting with several other students. Dixie is a woman who wants her life to make a difference. Working as a chaplain is one of those ways she is used in life-changing events. Be blessed by walking with her in this chapter as she ministers to one facing death. Here's Dixie …

My one-afternoon-a-week job as a chaplain-counselor in a Christian physician's office often brings me alongside people in life's most difficult crises. Sometimes, I'm blessed as much as the people I attempt to help.

When the doctor asked if I would visit Doris King, a patient in her mid-60s who was hospitalized with cancer, I felt uncertain how to help. Then I thought of my lap harp, a small version of the folk or Celtic harp.

I'd just begun lessons and knew only three songs, one of which was "Jesus Loves Me." I took my harp to the hospital room where I found Doris with her husband, Fred. He reminded me of a gentleman farmer, and Doris, with her white hair and soft, round face, looked like someone who could give good hugs. They were delighted with the little harp. They listened, misty-eyed, as I played and sang my short repertoire. Across the hall at the nurses' station, nurses also listened.

A year after that first meeting, Doris returned to the hospital and Fred asked if I could visit her again. That week, while preparing my Sunday sermon for the small church I pastored, I read James 5:14 (NIV): *"Is any one of you sick? He should call the elders of the church to pray over him and anoint him with oil in the name of the Lord."*

I presented a short version of my sermon to Doris. The concept of anointing with oil was new and fascinating to her. She said she felt very anxious about dying. "I don't want to leave Fred behind. I still have so much to do."

"Would you like me to anoint you?" I asked.

"Oh, yes."

I touched her forehead with oil and as we prayed together, she relaxed. Her face reflected peace. "I'm not afraid anymore," she reported.

I made a weekly appointment to visit Fred and Doris at their home, an hour's drive from where I live. Fred had removed the dining room table and set up a bed so Doris could supervise him in the kitchen and see who came in the front door. His tenderness impressed me.

Every week, the Lord gave me just the right thing to share with them. Early on, I gave them one of my favorite books, *To Heaven and Back,* by Rita Bennett. Rita tells of her husband's death and other true stories of people's Near-Death experiences. She shares the comfort she would like for herself and those around her if she were facing death.

Once I asked what worship songs Doris and Fred liked. Doris mentioned "How Great Thou Art." She mouthed the words, worshipping as I sang. Then Fred asked for his favorite modern chorus, "Shout to the Lord."

We also listened to CDs that I thought would bless them. One day on the way to their home, a new worship song sprang into my mind. I called my home phone and sang the composition into the answering machine so I wouldn't forget it, then sang it to them when I got there. They were delighted to be first to hear a brand-new song.

As her illness progressed, Doris's skin became dry and flaky. I brought cucumber-melon lotion and rubbed it on her thirsty hands and arms. "Have you ever had a foot massage?" I asked.

"No, never," she replied.

She thoroughly enjoyed the massage I gave her. "So, Fred," I said when I finished, "you've never given her a foot massage? I've started something here; now you're going to have to continue it."

Doris smiled and nodded agreement.

Since they'd enjoyed the lap harp in the hospital, I brought my big harp and played all the songs I'd learned in the past year.

They'd read *To Heaven and Back* and found out what the Bible said about Heaven. The Near-Death stories helped relieve them of the fear of dying. Reading the Scriptures the author suggested gave them a daily focus. They loved that. Even though they'd been in church all their lives until Doris got sick, they were hungry to read more of God's Word. When Fred saw my little electronic Bible, he went right out and bought one for himself.

When Doris told me how she missed going to church, I asked, "Would you like to have communion?"

"Oh, yes."

"At our church, I give it with a messianic emphasis. Would that be all right?"

They agreed, so I brought *matzah* bread, the four cups, and the grape juice and went through a Passover service with them. I excluded the big Passover meal but included all the symbolism present in communion: the cup of sanctification, the cup of deliverance, the cup of redemption, and the cup of praise. They loved it all.

Each time I visited, I prayed with them, and Doris always requested prayer for other people, never for herself.

Over the weeks, I had given sermons and music, brought lotions, played the harp, shared communion, and sung my new song. Then came a visit when I said, "I'm so sorry. I don't have anything to offer you this week."

"Yes, you do," they said. "You came, and we just want to visit with you. All week we look forward to your coming."

So I talked about my life, my children, and my struggles with our small congregation, and our cancelled mission trip to India. Fred told me, "Just think. If you'd gone to India, You'd not have been here for us."

At this point, our roles began to reverse. They were becoming the encouragers. Around this time, Doris and I approached the subject of her dying.

"Doris," I said, "some people would be angry that they're going through this. You don't seem to feel that way. You're so eager to learn more about the Lord, even though your body is failing."

She waved her hand and her expression seemed to say, "What a waste of time to be upset when I still have so much to live for."

The next time I visited, she seemed much weaker. She slept much of the time. She awoke, just wanting Fred near her, holding her hand. They talked about how they'd enjoyed their lives together and how blessed they were to have had one another. I felt privileged to share this tender time and when I saw Doris's tears, I cried, too.

Then she ran out of energy and couldn't speak anymore. Fred laid his head on the bed, still holding her hand, and wept huge sobs. The emotion of the moment wrung us both out.

After we recovered, I gave Fred a hug, said goodbye, and went to my office. But I needed comfort myself. Turning to my office manager, I burst into tears. She hugged me and prayed for me, giving me just the emotional support I needed.

During one of our visits, I had asked Doris, "May I play my harp at your memorial?"

Doris answered, "I would be honored if my friend would do that."

Another time, Doris seemed unaware of my presence, but I played my harp anyway. I told her family that when she began to take long, deep breaths, it would signal her soon departure, but to keep talking to her. Dying people are often aware of what's going on around them although they cannot respond. The family was glad to know this.

All too soon, Fred called to say that Doris had crossed into Heaven. At her memorial service, I played my harp for her. When time came to share memories of Doris, I felt privileged to tell that she taught me how to die. She had demonstrated how to go on living, right up to the end, with dignity and grace.

Pastor Dixie leaves us with some excellent "Tips to Help the Dying."

1. Don't be afraid to touch. Hug, hold a hand, and give a massage. Human touch is comforting.

2. Stimulate the spirit and the intellect with print or taped books, discussions, and sermons. People can learn and grow to the very end of life.

3. Enjoy music, poetry, and other art forms together.

4. Share the Scriptures.

5. Pray for and with patients and their families.

6. Encourage the person to talk about his/her feelings about death. If not a Christian, ask, "Are you ready?" Be prepared to show the way.

7. Share stories from your own life.

8. Don't be afraid to become emotionally involved.

9. Realize that you may need to ask for help for yourself, because you will grieve, too. Find someone to support you.

Author's Reflection, Dave's Story, and Psalm 23

What a beautiful message Dixie has given us. As you go on in life, you too may be at the bedside of a dying person. I know I have thus far been there for my father, my stepdaughter, my husband, and Dave Herivel.

How awesome it would be to have pastors prepared as Chaplain Dixie Nash to walk the last miles with their parishioners. The angels in Heaven must smile with joy as they see and hear her playing her harp to usher the dying into Heaven.

This segues to my friend Dianne Herivel, who was introduced in Chapter Three at her father's death. Later she walked through the last hours of her husband, Dave's life.

I had the privilege of joining her. I was invited by Dianne to accompany her to Dave's hospital room. He was semi-conscious and unable to speak. Dianne stood at his head on his right, I on the other side at his left. Dianne began the difficult, yet needful task of saying goodbye to Dave, her husband of twenty-seven years.

God was with her strengthening her all the way. She voiced her love for him and her gratitude for the years they shared together and for his love and care as a husband and a father. She held his hand and told him how much she would miss him, yet gave him permission to go, assuring him she would be all right. As Dianne looked up at me, it seemed my turn to speak. I did not know what I was going to say to him.

I stood by his bed and said, "Hi Dave." He couldn't move his head to look to the side or speak as he was on the life support of a ventilator. Although he could not look at me, I knew he could hear me. I continued, "I want to pray a prayer to help you on your journey, Dave." Suddenly I knew I was to pray the twenty-third Psalm personalized. Gently laying my hand on his shoulder, I began:

The Lord is Dave's Shepherd; he shall not want.
The Lord makes Dave lie down in green pastures. He

leads him beside the still waters. He restores Dave's soul. He leads him in the paths of righteousness for God's namesake. Yes, though Dave walks through the Valley of the Shadow of Death he will fear no evil, for God is with him. The Lord's rod and staff they comfort Dave.

You prepare a table before Your child in the presence of his enemies. You anoint Dave's head with anointing oil; his cup runs over. Surely goodness and mercy have followed Dave all the days of his life: And he will dwell in the House of the Lord, Forever. Amen.

Though Dave could not speak, his eyes looked over to his wife, Dianne at the other side of his bed. She explained to me, "He said, 'Thank You.'"

I was so overwhelmed with the Holy Spirit's presence that I could hardly stand up. How grateful I was for God's leading in that precious time.

I came back in later when Dianne's mother, daughters Emily and Jennifer, Dave's mom, and Dianne gathered at his bedside just before he died. Emily looked at Dianne and said softly, "Mom we have to sing." Dianne said to her quietly, "Emily, I don't know if I can." Emily replied, "Mom we have to."

So Emily and Dianne sang, *Be Thou My Vision*. Then they ended with a chanted version of the *Nunc Dimittis*, a setting of the *Song of Simeon*, after he had held baby Jesus and was now content to die. The words are:

Lord, now let Thy servant depart in peace, according to Thy Word. For mine eyes have seen Thy salvation, which Thou hast prepared before the face of all people. A light to lighten the Gentiles and the glory of Thy people, Israel. Glory be to the Father and to the Son and to the Holy Ghost. As it was in the beginning, is now, and ever shall be. World without end. Amen.

As they were singing, Dave's respiration gradually slowed and at the *Amen*, he took his last breath! The ICU nurse stood quietly by as a witness. She simply turned off the alarms on the respirator. It was a holy moment as his spirit left the room and entered the presence of the Lord. The Holy Spirit was orchestrating each and every moment.

Dave's pastor came in the room with the rest of the family. After a word of comfort, the family sang several lovely hymns as Dianne conducted them. I even joined in. I don't think that hospital and staff will ever be the same! Nor will any of us.

The Apostle Paul says of Christ, *"For He must reign till He has put all enemies under His His feet. The last enemy that will be destroyed is death"* (I Corinthians 15:25, 26). The twenty-third Psalm calls this serious valley of life, *"The valley of the shadow of death."* The fear of death is negated in this phrase, and that is true for all those who have accepted the Lord as their Good Shepherd. Jesus says to the crowd gathered round Him, *"Most assuredly, I say to you, if anyone keeps My word he shall never see death"* (John 8:51).

This being the truth of God's Word, neither Dave Herivel nor Doris King saw death. They were delivered out of death and into the arms of God.

Chapter Seven's Commentary
Coded Message at the Gates

Rita Bennett

The picture at the front of this chapter is a Bible code discovered as I was studying the list of the Tribes of Israel from the Book of Revelation. Having learned that Jewish names always have a meaning so I decided to look up the meaning of each Hebrew name.

I was impressed to research the Hebrew names of the Tribes of Israel and their meanings. I used the list of the Tribes as given in the concluding Book of the Bible (Revelation 7:5-8, 21:22). What I found amazed me. They actually made a most wonderful "Welcome Home" message as the weary traveler arrives at the Gate of Home. I only needed to add a few words to make complete phrases.

You'll be meeting famous martyrs through history. Your new family is unbelievably large. Everyone is humble and full of love. The feeling of peace is everywhere.

It became a true Message at the Gates from Scripture, a Bible Code if you will, and a message of healing, now opened and revealed for all of God's family. Since publication in 1997, God has let this Message At (or On) the Gates be read by at least 200,000 people and more at my web site. Some readers may have slipped right by this new insight, not realizing the awesomeness of this message at the Gates. Now with the picture to aid readers, it can be understood even better.

Twelve-Part Message At the Gates

Let's look at the twelve-part message at the Gates, again. It reads like this:

81

Confessors and praisers of God, looking upon the Son, a band of blessed ones, wrestling is over, forgetfulness of the pain, hearing and obeying His Word, cleaving to our Lord, Who is our reward, we are Home, we are added to the Family of Jesus, Son of the Father's right hand. (Bennett, 1997, p.115.)

The Code Revealed

We will not feel comfortable in Heaven unless we are *"Confessors and praisers of God."* Heaven will ring with hosannas and songs of praise. *"Viewing the Son,"* means because Jesus gave His life for us, we can hardly wait to see Him! We long to look upon His face, at last. We are *"a company"*—a family not an only child.

We are truly *"Blessed"* ones. What greater blessing can we have than being in the glorious presence of God forever? *"Wrestling"* is over with sin, sickness, temptation, demonic warfare, and more. *"Forgetfulness"* of pain on emotional, spiritual, and physical levels. *"Hearing and obeying"* God's Word is a primary key to entering the City of Light. In marriage, we cleave to our partner. Now in Heaven we are spiritually *"cleaving to"* our Lord Messiah, our Bridegroom, eternally.

Our Greatest Reward

He is our *"reward."* We desire no other gifts but God's presence. We are "Home." We made it! And what a Home. We are *"added to"* the family of Jesus. The Father, *Yahweh*, desired a family and sent His Son to earth that we might be born again, spiritually becoming God's children. *"Son of the right hand"* of the Father. Jesus Christ (Messiah) sits in honor at His Father's right hand at the Throne. Jesus gave His life for us so that all these gifts can be ours.

We are eternally grateful as we see this message revealed through the names of the twelve Tribes at the Gates of Heaven. This Bible Code is open to us even before we get there.

Relax with a Thankful Heart

Take a few moments to close your eyes, breathe in God's presence, relax with open hands, and picture this awesome Gate. Look up at the names of the Tribes and review the meanings of the names. Savor the message. See how many of the twelve parts you can recall and be thankful.

Remember how the awesome Pearl Door of the Gate will open for you. You too are a pearl of great price to God. The guarding Angel will be there to greet you. Family and friends are eager to visit with you. Loretta Jesse-Reed, Lou Hiett, Grandma Elizabeth Neil from Angel Place, Doris King, and Dave Herivel will be somewhere in the throng of your new family.

You are awesomely loved by Almighty God. One day you'll also meet the Father, the Son and Holy Spirit at the Throne.

You too will be welcomed Home. It is beyond your fondest dreams.

Map of the New Jerusalem

CHAPTER EIGHT

I Traveled at the Speed of Light

Cherie Calbom's Story

This is the first time I have ever publicly told my full story. Though I did not see Heaven, I was on my way, traveling at what seemed like the speed of light to twinkling lights in the distance. It was a place of perfect peace, from the moment I felt my spirit pop up and out of my body. I knew I had left everything here on earth and was on my way Home. It was so very peaceful.

Then, all of a sudden, I took a *giant* step back.

The Crisis

I was thirty-two, single, and heading back to school to finish my degree—Bachelor of Speech Communication—at Long Beach State University. To earn extra money for my education I took a housesitting job in a lovely Southern California neighborhood for vacationing family friends. I was happily working on my first book on the single life.

It was the Fourth of July and I had just returned from a barbecue at my boyfriend's home. It was midnight when I retired. I was shocked to wake up around 3 A.M. and see a strange young man with long brown hair in my bedroom crouched in a corner. I gasped at the sight. My movement revealed that I was awake and had seen him.

Like an animal, he leapt from his crouched position toward my bed. He attacked me with a heavy metal pipe, which I later learned from detectives was used for smoking dope. He beat me on the head repeatedly with the lead pipe; yelling, "Now you are dead!" and then he choked me until I was unconscious.

I felt what I now know was my spirit leaving and floating up and out of my body. Then all was still. I sensed I was traveling at what seemed like the speed of light through black space with twinkling lights in the distance.

As suddenly as I had left, however, I was suddenly back in my body, outside the house, clinging to a fence at the end of the dog run and screaming for help. I do not know how I got there.

The neighbor lady who knew me heard me screaming and sent her husband who carried me back to their home. They called the police and an ambulance. Without their help, I no doubt would have died at the secluded dog run location.

I suffered serious injuries to my head, neck, back, and right hand, with multiple head wounds and part of my scalp torn from my head. I also incurred numerous cracked teeth that resulted in several root canals and crowns. But my right hand sustained the most severe injuries, with two knuckles crushed to mere bone fragments that had to be held together by metal pins, and six months after the attack, I still could not use it. The cast I wore, with bands holding up my ring finger that was nearly torn from my hand, looked like something from a science-fiction movie.

I felt and looked worse than hopeless, with the top of my head shaved, red, swollen eyes, and a gash on my face, a useless right hand, terrorizing fear, and barely enough energy to get dressed when I awoke each morning.

It took every ounce of my will, faith, and trust in God, deep spiritual work, alternative medical help, extra vitamins and minerals, juicing vegetables and fruit, emotional release, healing prayer, and numerous detoxification programs to heal physically, mentally, and emotionally.

I met a nutritionally minded physician who had healed his own slow-mending broken bones with lots of vitamins and minerals and he gave me vitamin cocktail IVs. Juicing, cleansing, nutritional supplements, a nearly perfect vegan diet, and prayer, along with physical therapy, helped my bones and other injuries heal.

After following this regimen for about nine months, what my hand surgeon said would be impossible, my hand became fully restored and fully-functional. He had told me I'd never use my right hand again, and that it wasn't even possible to put in plastic knuckles because of its poor condition. But my knuckles did indeed re-form and function of my hand returned. A day came when he told me I was completely healed, and though the doctor admitted he did not believe in miracles, he did say, "You're the closest thing I've seen to one."

Healing My Trauma

Equally important in the restorative process was the healing of my soul—a place no one could determine the degree of injury. I experienced healing from the painful memories and trauma of the attack through prayer, laying-on of hands, and deep emotional healing work. It seemed like endless buckets of tears had been stored up in my soul from old wounds, such as my mother's death at age six, along with the attack. All that pain needed release.

A group that helped me a lot during my emotional recovery I call, "The Kitchen Angels." The "angels" are composed of a mother, daughter, and friend. When I had a need, I would call them and we would gather around their kitchen table and pray. For example, at night I often could not sleep because of the terror of that horrible attack on my life. One afternoon I shared this need with my praying friends.

One kind of prayer they used for me was called a "Prayer of Deliverance." They followed what Jesus did when He healed people and used some of the same words from the Bible. I recall them saying something like, "In Jesus' Name, I rebuke and bind the spirit of fear that attacked you during your ordeal and continues to harass you at night. You, spirit of fear, have no right to torment Cherie, this child of God. Be gone now and do not return! Amen."

After the deliverance prayer, they did a "Soul Healing Prayer" for the trauma by practicing the Presence of Jesus who is our omnipresent Lord. I went into the scene where He sent the neighborhood friends to rescue me. I was reminded in prayer that Jesus was there to help me and that He was grieving with me. He was the only one who could fully heal the wounds in my soul. He forgave all humanity on the Cross and only He could help me forgive this addicted, 17 year-old burglar.

Forgiveness and letting go came in stages and was an integral part of my total healing. I had to be honest about what I really felt and willing to face the pain and toxic emotions and let them go. But, finally, I was free. A time came when I could celebrate the Fourth of July (the anniversary of the attack) without fear.

I viewed the fireworks from the sailboat my husband John and I had rented with friends in 1987. I knew I was free! The red, white, and blue explosions in the sky seemed to be saying, "Celebrate your life. You are healed and whole to live your purpose."

Finally I knew more peace and health than I ever thought possible. I experienced what it was to feel *whole*—complete, not damaged, not broken, wounded, or impaired, but truly healed and restored to wholeness in body, soul, and spirit. And, I knew there was a purpose for my life—a reason I had lived. I could help others find their way to wholeness.

Author's Reflection

I met Cherie in 1984 at the Holiday Inn near the Seattle-Tacoma Airport. The event was an *Emotionally Free®* Conference of 500 people of all denominations and from different parts of the United States. My late husband, Dennis Bennett, was at that time Rector of St. Luke's Episcopal Church in Seattle and our church had organized this event where we were presenters.

Of course I did not realize that Cherie would meet her husband-to-be, John Calbom, at this conference. John lived in Kirkland, Washington and Cherie lived in Garden Grove, California. The conference and their interest in healing brought them together. Within six months of this event John and Cherie were married!

Without the *Emotionally Free®* Conference, Cherie and John said, "We might not have met." They invited Dennis and me to dinner soon after their marriage and let us know that they considered us to be their "matchmakers." What an honor.

As of 2008, the Calbom's ministry of wholeness has grown. For instance, Cherie has written over a dozen books on Nutritional Healing and Wholeness. Cherie has a M.S. degree from Bastyr University and John has a M.A. degree in Counseling Psychology from Santa Clara University. They have been on numerous television shows proclaiming wholeness and life's purpose.

This is a true story of how God can turn everything to good—when we give our lives over to Him, love and follow Him.

Chapter Eight's Commentary
Map of the New Jerusalem

Rita Bennett

Since we can only get a glimpse of Heaven, we show a map revealing that we're only seeing the East end of it. In this foursquare City, we can guess its North, South, and West entrances are similar to this one. It is most likely that all twelve of the entrances to Heaven will have the same beautiful boulevard view because at certain times people could be arriving at many different gates.

Cherie was headed towards Heaven, traveling through the star-studded heavens at the speed of light. She almost got to see the view of Heaven from the sky but it was not her time. God had and still has more for her to do on this beautiful blue planet called Earth.

Not only is Heaven described as being in a square shape but as we said earlier, what we are showing you in picture form is only one layer of the City. The Apostle John in Revelation tells us further that he saw Heaven as a cube in shape. This is reminiscent of the Old Testament Holy of Holies and Ark of the Covenant, both built in cubic shape according to God's command to Moses.

This gives Heaven, the City of God, a total size of 3,375,000,000 cubic miles! Such dimensions stagger our imaginations. Those who have studied Heaven's dimensions have guessed that it can house from 28 billion to 30 trillion people (Cornwall, 1989, p. 65). That means there will not be any property shortage for our wondrous Home above.

This is an awesome picture given by the Apostle John. He was caught up into Heaven in a vision, went on a Spirit-filled guided tour, and then wrote about it in his book called Revelation. John was so close to Jesus Christ while He was on earth, that I take his vision seriously. The Book of Revelation is the *Revelation of Jesus Christ* and the culmination of the Church and the Messianic Age.

Conversely, some Bible expositors think the Book of Revelation is simply symbolic or historic. Consider this, if John was not speaking from God's inspiration then how did he know two thousand years ago that the dimensions of Heaven he penned in Revelation would continue to be valid? How did he know that these dimensions would take care of all the people who lived and died previously right up to the present population of the world, and beyond? We can be sure that John did not have a calculator or computer!

It was God's knowledge and it came to the beloved apostle, Gospel writer John by revelation of the Holy Spirit. If you want to understand his book better, there are many excellent scholarly studies available today. Since we are living near the beginning of the Seventh Biblical Millennium, it is time for gaining more of God's awesome wisdom.

More revelations are ahead in **Part Two—*Jesus' Latest Words from Heaven.***

CHAPTER NINE

Cherubim Worship God

CHAPTER NINE

My Sister's Journey to Heaven

Shade O'Driscoll's Story

It was a cool clear Dallas morning, the sun just coming up on All Saints' Day, November 1, 2007. I slipped into the chapel on the assisted living campus as my sister, Jan was just seeing the beauty of Heaven and her Lord. Through my tears I thanked Father for the sister He gave me for all my seventy years.

She had said, "Shadie when you come to see me we'll go to the chapel together." Flying into Dallas the night before, my daughter, Sarah took me straight to Jan's bedside as she had already become unconscious two hours earlier. I sat beside her knowing her spirit was awake, singing the hymns of our childhood, praying, and reading God's words. Though we could not go to chapel, we worshipped together during those last hours.

As I looked upon her face, it was if I were looking on the face of an angel. Her suffering seemed to have melted away all the worldliness of this life. It was like I was already looking into the face of a child of Heaven.

In our most helpless moments we become as little children. Jesus said, *"Let the little children come to me, and do not forbid them; for of such is the Kingdom of Heaven"* (Matthew 19:14. KJV). Jesus also said, *"...whoever does not receive the Kingdom of God as a little child will by no means enter it"* (Mark 10:15,

KJV). We come to God as a little child. We brought nothing into this world and we shall take nothing out but the childlike faith in our Abba, our "Daddy-God" who loves us and will take us to Himself.

"Let Not Your Heart Be Troubled"

That same night our daughter, Mary in Seattle was awakened at 3 A.M. She began to pray asking God to save her Aunt Jan's life. She prayed desperately, but about 3:30 A.M. (5:30 Dallas time) Mary released her into Father's care and came to peace. Jan took her last breath on earth about that time. Proverbs 20:27 tells us that the spirit of man is the candle of the Lord. The Bible also tells us that at death our spirit returns to God who gave it. (See Ecclesiastes 12:7.)

Sarah and I went back to Jan's apartment and were with her son until the undertaker came to take the body away. When I looked this time upon her face, I surely knew her spirit was not there. I still loved that precious body that I had known from childhood. That body that I swam with on the beach in Florida, that I camped with on the riverbank in Arkansas, that I hunted deer with in the hill country of Texas, and yes, that body who had tried to comb my hair and dress me as a little girl when I wanted to be a tomboy!

I loved that body and did not want them to take it away, seemingly such a rude and shocking intrusion on a family love story. How could we give up and let strangers brusquely roll her body on a gurney and strap it down as if it were a piece of nothing. I knew she was not there; they were only taking away the shell she had lived in. But it seemed as if they were taking away a piece of my own heart. Jesus said, *"Let not your heart be troubled; you believe in God, believe also in me.... I will come again and receive you to myself; that where I am, there you may be also"* (John 14:1, 3, KJV).

We Were Not Made for Death

The plane lifted from the tarmac and headed north, as I looked down over Dallas. I felt I was leaving her, leaving the last place she was alive. Anger welled up in my heart and tears in my eyes, wetting the pillow hiding my face. Anger often comes with death because we were not made for death. Death truly is an ugly intruder on God's beautiful love story.

We were made for life. *"For the wages of sin is death, but the gift of God is eternal life in Christ Jesus our Lord"* (Romans 6:23, KJV). Eternity is for those who love. God is love, and He made us for Himself to live with Him and with those we love, forever in a beautiful place called Heaven. Though I knew I was going to see Jan again in Heaven, nevertheless, I was angry that I could never see her or talk with her again on earth.

As my tears soaked the pillow, God spoke in my spirit, assuaging my anger. "You are closer to her now than ever before, you are together in my Spirit."

"But God I am lonesome for her, I want to talk to her now, I want to share You with her as we did for so many years in those late night phone calls. I want to tell her a dozen things I've done through the day. We talked about our childhood days, about our mother and father, and we laughed at family jokes. Most of all we prayed together and believed.

"God, don't you know you did miracles for us when we prayed? You healed my immune disease, you dissolved the blood clot Jan had for more than a year. You took away the spot on her breast even before the second doctor could find out what it was. All of these things happened this year, why couldn't You have taken the cancer away when it returned?"

There are things we will not understand this side of Heaven, but one thing we can know, God cries our tears. In the 11th chapter of John we read how Jesus wept with Mary and Martha over the death of their brother Lazarus even though He knew He was going to raise him from the dead. His heart cries with us.

"Shadie, do it now; don't wait!"

Looking back, by late September and early October 2007, things were going terribly wrong. The gamma knife surgery had not seemed to help, but only made things worse. Jan was losing the ability to walk. She was confused at times and it was difficult to cope. Her family was finding it difficult to take care of her.

Even then, when she called me there was never any talk about dying but always living. However, she did say, "Shadie whatever you want to do in life, do it now; don't wait! There was authority in her voice that called forth response. My response was to straight-way sign up for art lessons. For years I had wanted to take watercolor lessons. Mother gave us all art lessons as children, but I had not had one since.

What a joy my lessons were. I told Jan about my first two simple paintings of a carrot and pepper. I couldn't wait to show them to her, and with excitement I carefully packed them the night before flying to Dallas. Though she never saw them on earth, perhaps she's seeing them now. The Bible tells us we are surrounded with a great cloud of witnesses (in Heaven). (See Hebrews 12:1.)

"Surely He Has Borne our Griefs ..."

When Jan was experiencing terrible pain the doctors did not realize the cancer had gone into the spine. During these days she called and said, " Shadie, I would like to have a crucifix. That might seem strange to you since I have been a Protestant all my life and have only viewed the empty cross. But now I need to hold the crucifix in my hands for I need to know Jesus is with me in my pain, and that He is feeling it as He felt it on the Cross."

This made sense to me because Jesus is now outside of time. In Heaven there is no time. Jesus can come into any moment of our earthly time whether it is the past, present, or future. So for Jan He was still on the Cross bearing her pain. *"Surely*

He has borne our griefs and carried our sorrows ..." (Isaiah 53:4, KJV).

Jan's oncologist went out of town during her last week. There was not proper communication and authority for her son to obtain pain medication nor could the hospice nurse. Both were obtained on her last day. But before she had the medication a puzzling thing happened. She cried out, "Don't whip Him," and then she said, "Don't whip me!" At first those who heard this did not know what was happening, later her son realized that she was identifying with the scourging of Jesus.

Indeed, the Lord did take the stripes on His back that we might be healed and Jan is healed forever. She will never again feel pain and God will wipe all tears from her eyes. "*... With His stripes we are healed*" (Isaiah 53:5, KJV). "*He will swallow up death in victory; and the Lord God will wipe away tears from off all faces ...*" (Isaiah 25:8, KJV).

Sweet Memories

The funeral was planned for Good Shepherd Methodist Church in Kansas City. We arrived two days before on a gorgeous Autumn morning, the sun beaming through the glass door prisms in Jan's Parkville, Missouri, home. Sarah and I and her son and family were all there. We were preparing for the "viewing" with old friends in St. Joseph, Missouri, where she had lived many years before.

It seemed strange and "out of place" to be in her home without her there. What a beautiful home, the home of an interior decorator, which was her degree from SMU, and the home of an artist. Her title was Missouri "artist in residence" which meant she could and did teach art in schools all over the state. The rooms were just as she had left them in August, having to leave quickly for Dallas where her oncologist was and where her son resided.

Walking through the house I lived again dozens of sweet memories; cooking together in the kitchen, talking about paintings in her studio, reading the Psalms and having devotions on the deck swing, planting the old antique rose in the garden. She was so much a part of her home, every room held memories of sweet times.

A Celebration of Life

Driving up to St. Joe I braced myself for what I dreaded, viewing death; but much to my surprise, walking into the Mierhoffer Funeral Home, I walked into a celebration of life! Jan's son had given Mr. Mierhoffer fifty photos of Jan including babyhood, childhood, high school, college, wedding, and many family and extended family pictures.

Entering the room where her casket stood, I heard music and saw on the wall a video show in progress, pictures of Jan radiantly alive. There were pictures of her with Mother and Daddy and even myself, pictures of that beautiful life my sister had lived. The room was filled with color, gorgeous bouquets amidst large easels holding the paintings Jan had painted this year. Instead of being sad, shockingly I was gloriously happy! I wanted to dance and shout and sing to all of her friends and myself, "She's not dead, she's alive!!!"

Yes, the body was there and her friend, Dorothy, had lovingly chosen for her to be dressed in a wedding suit which she had never worn. Some years after her husband Bill died, Ben, a retired doctor and gentle spirit came into her life giving joy and happiness. The wedding was planned, and the suit purchased, but the slow death of Alzheimer's stepped in. The wedding had to be canceled. Ben preceded Jan to Heaven a year before.

Dressed in her wedding suit, how appropriate, for now she is with her heavenly Bridegroom, the Lord Jesus awaiting the marriage supper of the Lamb. *"Blessed are they which are called unto the marriage supper of the Lamb"* (Revelation 19:9, KJV). In the Bible, Jesus is called the Lamb of God because He was and is the ultimate sacrifice on the Cross for the sins of mankind. Instead of lambs being sacrificed for sins, as was done for hundreds of years, Jesus died *"once to bear the sins for many"* (Hebrews 9:28a, KJV).

Until We Meet In Heaven

A couple of days before the viewing I tried but without success to find and buy a small Bible to put in Jan's hands in the coffin. That night before going to sleep I found her own small New Testament and Psalms in her bedroom bookcase. Opening it, I discovered that the front presentation page had never been inscribed. I took a pen and wrote:

To my precious sister, Jan,

Thank you for all you've done and for all you mean to me.

I love you.

Until we meet in heaven,

Shadie

Though her body will return to dust as will the Bible she holds, the Living Word, Jesus, will raise her dead body and Jan will have a new resurrected body that will never hurt again.

It is sown a natural body; it is raised a spiritual body ... And as we have borne the image of the earthly, we shall also bear the image of the heavenly.... In a moment, in the twinkling of an eye, at the last trump: for the trumpet shall sound, and the dead shall be raised incorruptible, and we shall be changed ... Death is swallowed up in victory ... thanks be to God which gives us the victory through our Lord Jesus Christ.
(I Corinthians 15:44, 49, 52, 54, 57, KJV)

Kevin, Jan's beloved assistant pastor, gave the funeral message. He shared his first memory of Jan. A few weeks after his arrival as the new assistant, Jan greeted him on a Sunday morning and in her Southern drawl said, "Kevin, how are ya comin?

He did not quite know what to make of that, but he replied, "I'm coming!" This was Jan's way of saying, "How are things going for you?"

In the service Kevin went on to say that Jan will probably greet us in Heaven with, "How are ya comin?" My reply until then is, "Jan, we're comin!

"You Can Do It"

Until then, until that grand and glorious moment when we too arrive on Heaven's shores, there is a legacy—a legacy that Jan left for all of us: "You can do it!" She believed with God's help you could do anything you needed to do and most things you wanted to do. Both with her words and actions, she lived this legacy for her son when he was failing architecture school; for me, her sister, when I was going through a tough time; and for her art students, especially the young teenage criminals in the institution where she sometimes taught.

As a six-year-old, she nearly died. It was before penicillin and ear tubes. Due to chronic ear infections she had to have a double mastoid surgery. This surgery entailed drilling into the mastoid bones on both sides of the skull. Though she spoke perfectly before the surgery, afterward she was left with the disability of stuttering. Tenaciously and by God's grace she overcame all the effects of that disability. She became a teacher, a Bible study leader, and often spoke publicly. Knowing this, the legacy Jan left us is all the more precious because, "She did it!" *"I can do all things through Christ which strengthens me"* (Philippians 4:13, KJV).

Autumn Leaves Blazing

After the funeral in Kansas City, the limousines took us on a four-hour drive across the state to a country cemetery near Lebanon, Missouri. This is where Jan's husband Bill is buried, and it is where the O'Quinns settled many years ago amongst the lovely rolling hills and farmland.

The day was glorious with autumn leaves blazing on the Missouri hillsides. Suddenly I realized we were on a familiar stretch of highway. Then I remembered when Jan had driven me to her condo on Lake of the Ozarks. The limousine crossed the lake and sure enough I looked back and saw the very buildings of the condo.

Four years ago after Jan's initial cancer surgery, she felt it was time to sell the condo. Along with her sister-in-law, June, I helped get it ready to sell. She loved that condo dearly; it was a refuge and a private retreat where she could paint to her heart's delight. In the mornings we sat on the porch swing reminiscing in the sunlight, and in the evenings we watched the lights on the gentle lapping water below.

Planning to Live not Die

Earlier this year on the Fourth of July, my family and I were on Friday Harbor in the San Juan Islands just getting ready to board a ferry when my cell phone rang. It was Jan. With great excitement she said, "Shadie, I have just bought another condo on the lake!" I could not believe it! We both were deliriously happy and immediately began planning when I would come to see the new condo. To myself, I thought, "My sister is not planning to die, she's planning to live."

Hours before she was to sign the closing papers on the condo, she and her friend, Kathy, were at the lake ordering furniture and planning each room. It was then that the doctor's call came saying the cancer had returned. Jan left Missouri and went to Dallas to her son's home.

Though she had to leave the condo on the lake, thanks be to God, a much more beautiful one that Jesus personally decorated just for her was waiting her arrival in Heaven. *"In my Father's house are many mansions:… I go to prepare a place for you"* (John 14:2, KJV).

In October, Jan's son secured an apartment on an assisted living campus. She could hardly wait to move in, and her friend,

Dorothy, came to Dallas to help her decorate the apartment. On next to the last day of her life Jan was directing Dorothy on how she wanted the curtains to be hung. Truly, she planned and loved life to the very end. She did not know that soon she would be in Father's house, the most glorious and beautiful place she had ever been or seen. *"... Eye has not seen, nor ear heard, neither have entered into the heart of man, the things which God has prepared for them that love him"* (I Corinthians 2:9, KJV).

Lamb's Book of Life

We arrived at the cemetery just as the sun was beginning to set. A strange happening occurred as the limos were driving through the gate. Jan's son noticed that one of the O'Quinn relatives waiting nearby had a stick and was beating the ground. He asked why, and the relative replied, "I was killing a snake."

Standing by the grave, I thought, why does such an unseemly and ugly thing like a snake have to happen now when we're just getting ready to commit Jan's body to the earth? Father God answered my question quickly. In my spirit I heard these words, "Satan's head is crushed, and he will never be able to hurt Jan again!" Tears came flooding up, and my soul was comforted. (The serpent is the symbol for God's enemy and our enemy, Satan.)

Friends and relatives were now gathering under the tent, soon dear Kevin would be saying the committal. I looked down at the vault in which the coffin would be placed and to my dismay I saw the words, JANICE O'GUINN instead of JANICE O'QUINN. "Oh no, don't they even know how to spell her name! On this earth can't we at least get the last word right?"

Again the response from Heaven was so quick. It was as if Jan and Father God were laughing together and He was telling me her words, "Shadie, don't worry about that, my name is spelled correctly in the Lamb's Book of Life, and that is where it really matters." Revelation 21:27 tells us that only those who are written in the Lamb's Book of Life shall enter Heaven.

After many hours we arrived back in Kansas City at midnight. A cold wind blew away our warm autumn day. The chill in the air told us winter had come. Though winter comes to all of us, God has spring on the way, the resurrection and new life. *"Jesus said,... I am the resurrection and the life: he that believes in me, though he were dead, yet shall he live: And whosoever lives and believes in me shall never die"* (John 11:25, 26, KJV).

On Tiptoes For Something More

As a little girl Jan often walked on her tiptoes. It was as if she were reaching for something higher. In this life we all are reaching for something higher. Intuitively we know there must be something more than this present life. We can never be fully satisfied here because God has made us for something so much higher and better. That place is Heaven. Jan is there now.

If you are saying, "How do I get there?" Jesus is the way, and there is no better time than right now—to ask Him to come into your heart and to forgive your sins. His forgiveness is a free gift.

Then you're on your way to a new life, a new love, and to Heaven ...

Author's Reflection

Shade O'Driscoll and I have been friends since the early 1960s. We met at a CFO Camp held at Allison Wells, in Jackson, Mississippi, where my brother, Bill Reed, M.D. was a guest speaker. I came from Florida and she from Arkansas and the Holy Spirit sealed our friendship for all these years. One year after Dennis Bennett and I were married in 1966, Shade's husband, Dick O'Driscoll, became one of the clergy at our church; St. Luke's Episcopal, Seattle.

Shade and I were in for a lot of adventures together from that time on including sharing together in this Ninth Chapter of *Heaven Tours.* Shade and Dick, now retired, have six wonderful children and many lovely grandchildren.[13]

Chapter Nine's Commentary
Cherubim Worship God

Rita Bennett

Sally's drawing of the six-winged cherubim who surround the Throne of God is lovely. The cherubim have the most holy work of worshipping at God's Throne, which is at the center of Heaven, and possibly the center of the universe.

These are not four beasts as the King James translation states it, but these are four cherubim whose natures are symbolized in picture form: brave as a lion, strong servant like an ox, as a wise human being, and as a swift, far-seeing eagle. Some Bible translators believe that these four angel beings have the actual faces of those four natures. The New King James translation calls them "living creatures." A single angel of this kind is called a cherub; *im* added makes it plural.

When one day in Heaven you look at the four living angelic creatures, you will be reminded of important biblical history on earth.

The Zondervan Pictorial Bible Dictionary tells us: "Primarily the cherubim are the living chariot or carriers of God when appearing to men: His throne or the bearers of it. Their earliest recorded employment was as guardians of Eden" (Tenney, Ed., 1967, p. 154). Moses was directed by God to place two cherubim of beaten gold on the mercy seat above the ark, where God would meet with Moses in the tabernacle (Exodus 25:18-22). What places of honor they hold.

"Rabbinical tradition assigns them [cherubim] to the standards of the divisions in the camp of Israel;

• the lion, Judah, on the East;
• the ox, Ephraim, West;

- a man, Reuben, South;
- the eagle, Dan, North.

Thus the standards, leading the Israelites, would indicate Israel as the earthly counterpart of the heavenly host, led by the cherubim" (Tenney, Ibid.).

Have you have ever studied the history of Israel: coming out of Egyptian bondage, led through the Red Sea, spending forty days at Mount Sinai where Moses received the Ten Commandments? Do you remember how a million Jews, with strangers among them, traveled in formation through the wilderness for four decades? If so, you will be excited to see these faces of the living creatures and what they mean.

You will be reminded of the study of the *Tabernacle in the Wilderness* that is also fascinating, and spiritually empowering. I recommend this study to help you understand the Old Testament more fully with all its unique biblical types and shadows. The men—Judah, Ephraim, Reuben, and Dan—each led by one of the four cherubim, and the leaders were each responsible for the wellbeing of three of the Tribes of Israel as they traveled.

Jesus is strongly represented in the Tribes and in the faces of the cherubim. For instance, the Tribe in the East, that represents the famous Eastern Gate of Heaven, is Judah. Jesus is of the Tribe of Judah. He is also called the Lion of Judah, and one cherub has the face of a lion. Judah also appropriately means praise. *"Let everything that has breath praise the LORD"* (Psalm 150:6).

Y'hudah is Hebrew for Judah. *Y'hudim* is the Hebrew name of the Jews.

The twelve Tribes encamped for the night in four groups of three: East, West, South and North. If seen from an aerial view, it would make the redemptive sign of the Cross of Jesus.

The plan for Jesus the Christ (Messiah) to redeem the world was set in place from before the foundation of the world. Father

God, the archangels, cherubim, seraphim, and all ranks of angels could look over the corridors of Heaven and see a blueprint of God's plan coming to pass. It was a view of the glory of God to come.

The Early Church Fathers
Early church fathers equated the four faces with the four Evangelists:
- Matthew, the lion;
- Mark, the ox;
- Luke, the man;
- John, the eagle" (Tenney, Ibid.).

Not only are believing Jews honored by the twelve Tribes connection with the faces and character of the cherubim, but believing Gentiles are also honored by being connected with the four Evangelistic Gospel Writers.

Summing it up
Summing up: "The cherubim are the bearers of the judgments which follow the breaking of the first four seals. They are significant in prophecy, and in the Apocalypse.... Their service is rendered immediately to God. They never come closer to man than when one took fire in his hand and gave it into the hands of *'the man clothed with linen'* (Ezekiel 10:7). Yet it is *'between the cherubim'* that lay the mercy seat on which the blood of atonement was sprinkled; nothing can more nearly touch our salvation" (Tenney, Ed., 1963-67, p. 154).

Some of those who have been written about in this book are already in the New Jerusalem: Loretta, Lou, Grandma Phelps, Doris, Dave, and Jan O'Quinn. They will be in the presence of the cherubim and know far more about them than we can this side of Heaven.

And seeing the Lion, Ox, Man, and Eagle they will be reminded of their own time on earth where they:

• praised God the Son—the Lion of Judah,

• served God—who is mighty with strength—typified by the Ox metaphor,

• studied to be wise like Jesus—who is fully God and fully Man joined forever, and

• waited on the Lord—to renew their strength as the Eagle.

Most of all they will know and experience our one true God, *Yahweh*: Father, Son, and Holy Spirit. One day we'll join them, but meanwhile there is more to learn and do for our almighty God and His Kingdom here on earth.

Majestic Throne of God

Divine Appointment at a Cemetery

Rita Bennett

My afternoon on December 26, 2001, began by attending a funeral for Fred Bailey from St. Alban's Episcopal Church. During the service, there was a time for family and friends to share their special memories with Fred.

I gave a brief testimony that as a Eucharist Bearer, taking the Lord's Supper to the homebound, I had visited Fred and his daughter, Susan, a number of times over the months. I told the congregation that near the end of his life, we had talked openly about Heaven and I had showed him the illustrations the artist, Sally Moser, and I had developed.

During the time in the service where we *Passed the Peace*, I remembered that I had a set of Heaven picture postcards that Pat, my graphics designer, and I had created at my office at Christian Renewal Association. With the size of Heaven being so massive, I used to think how unbelievable it was for my staff and I to put our seven pictures of Heaven on seven postcards! But here they were, conveniently tucked away in my purse. Not many people carry Heaven in their purse! I felt I should give them to Fred's daughter.

When I did, Susan's sister-in-law who was standing there, said she found my sharing the pictures about Heaven fascinating.

I told her I had given Susan these Heaven illustrations to share with the family, so she could see them again.

I enjoyed several other opportunities to comfort people during the reception, which kept me there longer than I had expected.

A Strange Meeting

As soon as I could, I walked to my little blue Honda station wagon in the parking lot and drove to the cemetery to take a large red Christmas Poinsettia for Dennis's grave. I arrived about 5:45 P.M. and it was getting quite dark in the early winter months. Since the gates close at dusk, I was happy and pleasantly surprised to find them still open.

As I drove up the little road, I saw a very tall man standing near where I was going to park. I was cautious and thankful at the same time. Rolling down my window I said, "Hello, do I have time to leave some flowers?"

He said, "Yes, I'm the caretaker. I have a good strong flashlight you can use if you didn't bring one."

Feeling somewhat assured, I said "Oh yes, I'd appreciate that." I was hoping very much that he really was the caretaker of this dark, shadowy cemetery!

I counted four large oak trees as I drove up the steep hill, parked the car, put on the emergency brake, and left the car lights on. The man joined me, introducing himself as Louie *(pseudonym)*. I opened the door to step out on the asphalt driveway.

I then opened the door to the backseat to retrieve items for my cemetery visit. He offered to help me carry the plant to the gravesite. Furthermore, he also wanted to assist me in setting up the plant when we got there. This was assuring.

I showed him how to place the broken and re-bent clothes hanger ends on both sides of the plant into the grass to keep it stable. I had learned how to do this from Dennis, when many times over the years we had visited the cemetery together.

Prayer and Introductions

While kneeling there on a rubber cushion I brought, I prayed aloud, "Father, please tell Dennis, Elberta, and Margi (Dennis's daughter) that I love them and I'm thinking about them on this very special day. Thank you, Lord. Amen." (I thought, *the caretaker might not like me praying so I'd better make this brief.*)

I got up and said as I looked at the headstones, "This is my late husband, Dennis Bennett, an Episcopal Clergyman, and to the left is Elberta, his first wife, and I am Rita, his second wife."

He nodded as if to say, "I see."

"And Dennis's oldest child, Margie, is buried just one row down, and a few plots over."

I mused; *this is quite an interesting cemetery introduction!*

A Revealing Conversation

The evening fog was flowing in under the pine trees as Louie walked me back to the car. Now he spoke quite definitely to me and I noticed a slight foreign accent, "I am an atheist. The Bible is full of lies, and I do not believe in heaven or hell. But I do believe in reincarnation and that life will go on."

I was gulping back my astonishment from his pronouncements. I tried to find a positive point of agreement to respond to him and said, "I agree with you Louie that life will indeed go on, yet I believe that we have to choose where we will live in that next life." (See Hebrews 9:27.)

I said further, "The Bible is the most wonderful book ever written and I am presently studying it in the original language of Hebrew, as it seems to me that is the best way to get back to what God originally intended us to know."

"And Louie," I continued, "the Bible has been tested more than any other book and survived over 3,500 years. It is so important to take time to study the Scripture. It reveals that

God loves you and has great plans for you now and through eternity."

I was very cold so I got into my car and rolled down the window to finish our conversation.

The caretaker responded further with quite a number of concepts, which revealed that he was into conspiracy theories. He was mad at the government, past presidents, the democrats and republicans, and much more.

The Bottom Line

I finally said, "Louie, let me tell you the bottom line. It is that Jesus Christ, the Prince of Peace, is coming back with His army of saints to straighten out this world."

A slight smile began to show on his face. "Will our presidents be judged?" he asked.

"Yes, they will," I assured him. He definitely liked this idea.

We were both shivering as we talked, the damp night air wrapping itself around us like a shroud. I knew I was going to have to bring this conversation to a close.

I said, "When you die, Louie, you will be met by Jesus Christ who will have nail pierced hands. When you see Him, please say, 'Yes!' and you can tell Him 'Rita Bennett sent you.'"

He looked at me intensely and had nothing more to say, except he pointed in the direction of his office and invited me to visit him there sometime. (I felt this was more of a man's job to take it from here. I prayed in my heart that Louie would receive Jesus as Lord sooner, rather than later.)

I gave him a copy of my organization's most recent newsletter called, *In Touch and Emotionally Free,* and told him to check out my web site *EmotionallyFree.org* that had some pictures of Heaven on it. He was willing to take the newsletter as we said goodbye. I considered that Louie could contact my office by e-mail or phone if he wanted further discussion.

Starting the motor, I drove up and around the cemetery's circular driveway, and out through the huge iron gates, my heart rejoicing. I'd never had such an exciting time at a cemetery! I wondered if the Holy Spirit might let Dennis know of my "divine appointment."

I had a chance to witness to an atheist right there in front of Dennis's cemetery plot! God was still working through Dennis, even though he had ten years before graduated to His heavenly Home.

Chapter Ten's Commentary
Majestic Throne of God

Rita Bennett

The throne scene is the most complex illustration of all. It is hard to even conceptualize the throne of God, but Sally and I have done our best to create something biblically sound but uniquely inspired by the Word and the Holy Spirit.

In the last *Heaven Tours* picture you saw the four Cherubim around the Throne of God. Now we have the enlarged picture of the throne Scene.

When designing the throne I chose to make it in three parts but joined together as one. We see Jesus to the right of His Father and the Greek letters representing the words Alpha and, across from it, Omega. Jesus is the only human form of God we humans can envision. I chose Light and the name I AM to represent our Father, and a dove to represent the Holy Spirit.

Alpha and Omega

The Greek letters on the throne, Alpha and Omega, are to remind us of God's omniscience. The Lord says, "I am Alpha and Omega, the beginning and the end, the first and the last" (Revelation 22:13). This statement or variations of it are quoted three times in Revelation and three times in Isaiah. In fact, God is not only the first and last letters of the whole Greek alphabet but all the letters in between.

In keeping with the Hebrew theme, we would say Jesus *(Yeshua)* is the Aleph and the Tav, the beginning and end represented by the Hebrew Alphabet. *Aleph* means first and strong. The letter *Tav* means a sign or a cross. In the earlier Phoenician alphabet *Tav* looks like a cross at a slight right angle. Historically, this is where the idea of signing a person with a cross on their forehead comes from. (See Ezekiel 9:4, *Spirit-Filled Life Bible*.)

Whatever language you speak, you can insert its first and last letters to personalize this truth of our Lord being the beginning and the end.

In Revelation 1:8, of Christ we read, "I am the Alpha and the Omega, the Beginning and the End," says the Lord, "who is, and who was, and who is to come, the Almighty." When He says, 'The Almighty," He admits His divinity.

I love to sing: "Who is, and who was, and who is to come." He is God past, present, and future all at once. Our Lord is now, was in the past, and will be in the future. He is the Omnipresent, timeless God. That is why here on earth we can pray about past, present, and future and see God work mightily. God is outside of time.

I AM

On the Throne in the middle to represent Father God, I chose the words I AM. When Moses was asked by God to go to Egypt to release the Children of Israel from bondage, Moses said:

> "When I come to the children of Israel and say to them, 'The God of your fathers has sent me to you,' and they say to me, 'What is His name?' what shall I say to them?"
>
> And God said to Moses, "I AM WHO I AM." And He said, "Thus you shall say to the children of Israel, 'I AM has sent me to you.'" (Exodus 3:13-14)

I Am Who I Am means, "I am the Self-existent One; the Eternal, the One who always has been and always will be (Psalm 90:2). It is equivalent to Jehovah [*Yahweh*] the Eternal" (Dake's A.R. Bible, p. 67).

The Dove

For the Throne to the right, I chose the symbol of the Dove. The dear Holy Spirit is gentle as a dove. Jesus says to His disciples, "Behold, I send you forth as sheep in the midst of wolves: be ye therefore wise as serpents, and harmless as doves" (Matthew 10:16). Here the Lord may be contrasting the wiliness of the Enemy with the gentleness of the Spirit.

He also is represented by flames of fire on the heads of the first Pentecost congregation in Jerusalem. He is also spoken of as spiritual rain, water springing up within believers, water to swim in. The One who fills our cup to overflowing. The Glory cloud over the children of Israel is the work of the Holy Spirit as they traveled toward the Promised Land of Israel. Any of these symbols would be biblical.

Eternal Now

This is the way Gerard Landry, M.D., a Death and Return *Experiencer*, described what happened when he died:

The first awareness was of eternity. How can I describe eternity to you? I'll give you an example. Our time dimension was created by God when He created the world. We need time to help us function properly. We need sleep to help rejuvenate our bodies.

For thousands of years, time was measured by sunrise and sunset. Humankind then developed various ways to tell time from the study of the heavens, to sundials, and clocks. Then came the wristwatch, which has become increasingly sophisticated. Now we have digital watches.

At one time, the measurement of time in seconds was unknown to us. Now seconds are broken into fractions, even to one billionth of a second called a nanosecond. That is faster than you can blink an eye. What we did not know in the past has now become known to us through inventions coming from study in the fields of physics and mathematics. Calculations of computer scientists are amazing.

Such inventions can also bring us to a greater understanding of eternity. For instance, we measure time by hours, minutes, seconds, microseconds, and nanoseconds. When we die, everything stops. It is like finally getting to the nanosecond, where time stops for us. Like a watch, our body stops at that time. Yet our spirit and consciousness continue to live on in a dimension beyond sequential time.

We go beyond nanoseconds into a space-time measurement we cannot know here on earth. I call it the eternal now, because that is how it felt to me. The past, present, and future are all merged into what Scripture calls eternity. Eternity is the present, the now that never ends.

Truly understanding this dimension requires a joining of the human spirit to the Holy Spirit. As this connection happens, we go beyond head knowledge to heart experience. Jesus came expressly to give us this kind of life—eternal life. He told us about it. He demonstrated it. He imparted it (Bennett, R., *A Doctor's Story*, p. 60, 61).

The Twenty-four Elders

Sally Moser designed golden thrones and rooms for the 24 elders who are seated around God's Throne. Let's see what the Scripture says about these 24 men of God.

The Apostle John is speaking:

"Immediately I was in the Spirit; and behold, a throne set in Heaven, and One sat on the throne. And He who sat there was like a jasper and a sardius stone in appearance; and there was a rainbow around the throne, in appearance like an emerald. Around the throne were twenty-four thrones, and on the thrones I saw twenty-

four elders sitting, clothed in white robes, and they had crowns of gold on their heads" (Revelation 4:2-4).

The Spirit-filled Life Bible describes them as, "The celestial representatives of all the redeemed, glorified, and enthroned, who worship continuously. White robes symbolize purity. The crowns suggest victory and joy, not political authority" (Revelation 4, footnotes, p.1967).

Who are the Elders?

The Jewish New Testament Commentary gives four possibilities of who the elders might be. I am drawn to the second one: "The twelve emissaries [Apostles] of *Yeshua* [Jesus] plus the twelve founders of the tribes of Israel; if so, they represent all of redeemed humanity" (Stern, 1992, p. 805).

On Mount Sinai God gave Moses detailed instructions on how He wanted the Tent of meeting in the wilderness to be built. There are six pieces of furniture: the Ark of the Covenant, the top of which was of beaten gold and above it two cherubim of gold facing one another overshadowing the mercy seat. Within the Ark were the golden pot of manna, Aaron's rod that budded, and the tables of the covenant. These were within the curtain of the Holy of Holies.

The Tabernacle in the Wilderness

In front of the curtain in the Holy Place was the golden Altar of Incense, which represented the prayers of the saints. Also in this location are the 12 loaves Bread of the Covenant, representing the 12 tribes. Next is the large gold Menorah composed of seven lamps, as today, they would be candles rather than wicks and oil.

In the Outer Court was the brazen altar of sacrifice. This was where animal sacrifices were offered. This altar represents the one and only perfect and everlasting sacrifice, Jesus the Christ. *"And as it is appointed for men to die once, but after this the judgment, so Christ was offered once to bear the sins of many. To those who eagerly wait for Him He will appear a second time, apart from sin, for salvation"* (Hebrews 9:27, 28).

In the Temple of Heaven Now

Of the six Temple furnishings, in Revelation only the gold Ark of the Covenant that includes the gold Mercy Seat, the gold seven-branched Menorah, and the Altar of Incense are mentioned. (See Revelation 11:19; 1:12, 13; 8:3.) I'll be sharing more about the gold Menorah or Candlesticks in Part Two.

The sea of glass could represent the Brazen Laver of God's Word. So that piece of heavenly furniture is represented here and if so, that represents the fourth piece of furniture.

The sea or river issues from beneath the Throne of God. This is the location where the redeemed will receive judgment for their works on earth. It is where we receive rewards, few, or many, and in essence are a part of judging ourselves as we look at our own reflection in the glass-like sea. Everyone at this *Bema* (Gr.) Seat, literally meaning Judgment Seat, already has his or her name written in the Lamb's Book of Life. (See Romans 14:10-12.)

His Train Filled the Temple

In the year King Uzziah died the prophet Isaiah had a vision of, *"the Lord sitting upon a throne, high and lifted up, and his train filled the temple"* (Isaiah 6:1). We do not know the temple spoken of here but some biblical scholars like Finis Dake believe it could have been a vision of Solomon's Temple on earth and the room is the Holy of Holies. (Dake, 1963, p. 685). This is the reason Sally Moser added the mauve colored train to our Lord's picture.

Other details about the Throne we'll have to wait to know, after we finish our journey on earth. We do at least have a good start. A well-known Heaven Scripture says, *"Eye has not seen, nor ear heard, nor entered into the heart of man, the things which God has prepared for those who love Him. But God has revealed them to us through His Spirit* (1 Corinthians 2:9-10).

Yes, of course we have seen and learned quite a bit on the tour thus far, but what we will actually see when we arrive could make this seem like Grade School in comparison. However, there is a great blessing for those who desire to plumb the depths of God's Word on this subject in advance. I've found it so.

Redeemer, Great High Priest, King

CHAPTER ELEVEN

Courts of Heaven Give Second Chance

Forrest Messenger's Story

I met Forrest in 2008 and it was all because of a picture on my friend Anita's wall. But that's getting ahead of the story. Here we go with Forrest's message.

When I was six years-old, my parents were for some reason wrapped in the turmoil of an unfriendly divorce. My father was a very ordered and controlling person and after the divorce was final, he lived a very different kind of life than we did at home.

Dad was a professional librarian, my mom, after feeling traumatized by ten years of living with a controlling husband, married a very easygoing musician, and soon they were part of the hippy culture of the 1960s.

I didn't choose to follow their lead; instead my role model was Dad. He had a roommate with whom he acquired a brand new home and bought everything he wanted, it seemed. He was constantly acquiring new furniture, driving new cars purchased every few years and taking my sister and me to an Episcopalian church every Sunday. We spent the weekend at his house every other week until he left Southern California to return to the Bay Area, which he loved dearly over Southern California, which he disdained.

I emulated who I thought my dad was by working hard and excelling in school and avoiding the hippy persona of my mom and stepdad at all costs while growing up in Orange County. All my friends' families looked like the Cleavers or the family in *Father Knows Best*. Their families were stable with both parents in the home and only the man worked outside the home.

After Dad moved to the Bay Area, I continued to go to church on my own but I didn't read the Bible and was not a born again Christian. In fact, after people in the Episcopalian church I went to on my own (riding my bike three or four miles each way) started getting "born again" and challenging me to do the same, I went back to the Catholic church which our family left after the divorce occurred.

I was hungry for meaning in life but frightened by what the Jesus Movement looked like. There wasn't anyone in my family who could explain to me who Jesus was, or why and if, I might want to consider allowing Him into my life.

It wasn't until I was 15 that I recognized how hard I had been working to keep any possible vestiges of a traditional lifestyle going for myself. That summer, my sister and I went camping with my dad and his roommate and my godmother's son, Richard, who was my age. After a couple of days, Richard revealed to me that the reason behind my parents' divorce was that Dad's roommate was his boyfriend. I couldn't have been more devastated.

I suddenly realized that I had been molested by his roommate from the age of eight to ten, and that Dad's outward persona of traditional values and orderliness was an empty shell. This was really too much for me to deal with at the time so I "borrowed" some pot from my mom and stepdad and began getting stoned for the next two years.

Getting stoned eventually became more than just a recreational experience for me. It became part of a search for true spirituality. By this time, Mom had gotten involved with Metaphysics and would take me to "psychic fairs." At one such event I watched a woman channel a spirit that spun her head around and through her voice gave psychic readings to the people present. I had cut my hand badly earlier that day and after leaving the meeting my one-inch cut was *completely healed over*. These experiences with my mom made me think that drugs were a potential door into the spirit world.

A family friend, who was a couple of years older than I was, began getting stoned with me and he introduced me to the writings of Alistair Crowley, a man who was into witchcraft. My friend Steven and I began to pursue the spiritual dimension of drug use together. One day Steven suggested that we sit in a meditative posture after we took some LSD. So we assumed a yoga posture, closed our eyes and endeavored to empty our minds of ourselves.

Soon I found myself hurtling through a dark tunnel towards a small light far away. There was a deafening roar that filled everything—it was like being next to a huge waterfall. The sound was overwhelming and everywhere. At the same time, I could see pictures on the sides of this tunnel from my short life—memories of people and events. My journey continued onward through this tunnel toward the light, which became larger as I approached it, while at the same time the roaring sound became louder and louder.

Eventually the light became large enough that I entered it. Having passed through the tunnel, I found that I was in a space or platform somewhere above the room where I started this process. The roaring sound ceased completely and my mind, emotions, and spirit felt a deep peace I had never experienced before. I looked down from where I was and could see my body down on the floor of my room where I started the journey.

My personal sense of serenity was short-lived, however. I turned around and was in the presence of a group of men who were like what I had heard of the descriptions of angels, only without wings. There were a good number of them, more than fifteen and less than thirty, but I was not in the mood to count them. The men were in this light space I had entered and I sensed that they had full insight into who I was. They recognized me even though I did not know who they were. The journey lost its luster for me as we spoke. In the light of their insight about me, and the questions they asked me, I suddenly felt exposed and vulnerable.

They asked me, "Are you ready to be dealt with, or do you want to go back to Earth and complete what you've left undone?" Their question and their piercing insight into my being made me see, in what felt like an instant, that to remain and be dealt with would be horrible. That was because I could see the terribleness of my own soul in a way I never had before. They did not see me as a victim, even though I had been victimized.

They saw, and I did too, that I was responsible for my own decisions. They knew that enough of the decisions I had made in the last few years had left me in a state vulnerable to some sort of complete and total judgment. I realized that I was unworthy at this time to be able to remain in this pure place I found myself in. So, in what seemed like an instant of being asked whether I chose to stay or go, I knew I truly had no other alternative than to go back and find out what I had left undone.

I was back in my body instantaneously, and Steven was back from wherever he went as well. The strange thing was that I was stone cold sober after having taken the LSD only two hours earlier. Normally, LSD leaves you pretty stoned for six to eight hours. This was different. I was in shock over what I had seen about myself and about the place I had gone after leaving my body. I now knew that I was not ready to die or pass through to the spirit world—that there was accountability for my life that I could not yet stand under.

Rita Bennett's Interview with Forrest Messenger:

After reading Forrest's dynamic testimony, I interviewed him via email:

Rita Bennett: Do you believe that you were having an NDE or (Death and Return—another way of saying it) experience during the time that you saw your body on the floor?
Forrest Messenger, CPA: Yes … I was given a choice to die or live and get my life straightened out.

Rita Bennett: Did your fear of dying change after this NDE experience?
Forrest Messenger: No, it increased. I did not become a Christian for another two years. I was unaware until this time of the gravity of accountability for my life actions.

Rita Bennett: What was your first step of faith after your return to your body?
Forrest Messenger: I had had some experiences on drugs prior to this one wherein God spoke to me and said directly that I did not need to take drugs to know Him. I rebutted His offer by telling Him that then I would not be able to turn Him off when I did not want Him around.

Rita Bennett: Did you repent?
Forrest Messenger: Prior to the NDE, my drug experiences felt like a progressive spiritual journey. The NDE stopped me in my tracks. I took LSD one or two more times and the last time I took it, a short spirit showed up in my room, and it looked kind of like a hobbit. But that's where the fun ended. I had lost my sense of clarity about good and evil by this time because of my involvement in the Occult. But this spirit felt

overwhelmingly evil. I sensed that he wanted to do me terrible harm and that he wanted to inhabit/control me.

It was after this experience that I began looking for a way out of the drug scene and within a month, I was clean and sober. But quitting drugs came through self-will and determination. What brought me to my knees was a girlfriend with whom I lived for a while. She was controlling and emotionally critical, if not abusive. I found that I was hanging onto the relationship for sex and felt powerless to change.

On Easter Sunday, 1980, I attended a service where the pastor said that when Christ died He buried sin in the grave and when He rose from the dead His resurrection gave us the power to live a life free from sin. I accepted that offer and was born again.

* * *

Rita Bennett: How do you feel about dying now? Afraid? Peaceful? Okay? Better than before?

Forrest Messenger: I fear how it might happen, because I don't like pain, but because of my relationship with Jesus I am not afraid of judgment or eternity. I already have eternal life.

Rita Bennett: What happened to your friend who took LSD with you? Where is he today?

Forrest Messenger: He became a private detective and lives in Southern California, the last I heard.

Rita Bennett: How is your spiritual life now?

Forrest Messenger: Good.

Rita Bennett: Is this the first time you will have given this particular experience publicly?

Forrest Messenger: I have shared it with people I know.

Rita Bennett: How do you feel about God's grace to you in giving you a "second chance?"

Forrest Messenger: God has been better to me than I deserve. I believe I am only here because He had a better plan and purpose for my life. For the past twenty-three years, I have been involved in leadership in my church through small groups, choir, serving in the young adult and youth departments of University Presbyterian Church and now Westgate Chapel.

Rita Bennett: Would you advise anyone to try LSD, or other drugs to find God?

Forrest Messenger: No way.

Rita Bennett: What is wrong with going to a medium for guidance or healing (regarding your cut on the arm healing fast).

Forrest Messenger: There are different kinds of spirits. I was unaware of this at the time. Any spirit that does not acknowledge Jesus Christ is not a good one. Mediums do not serve Jesus and the spirits they conjure up can be destructive, leading to bondage to drugs, bad relationships, alcoholism and even death.

Rita Bennett: Through prayer, did you renounce your experience of going to the medium?

Forrest Messenger: Yes, I have. For a while after quitting drug use, evil spirits showed up to taunt me (like a couple of years later after I became a Christian) and I prayed against them in the name of Jesus and they ceased.

Rita Bennett: Do you think it is important for a person to renounce witchcraft reading materials and participating in concepts learned in this Wicca belief system?

Forrest Messenger: Yes, I burned all of my Tarot Cards and magic books after accepting Christ.

Rita Bennett: Do you believe in Deliverance Prayer to cleanse oneself from stepping into occult practices?
Forrest Messenger: Yes.

Rita Bennett: Did you have this ministry?
Forrest Messenger: I have only exercised it for myself. I have not had other opportunities.

Rita Bennett: How was the communication from the Elders or the Angels [during your NDE] transmitted to you? Were they in words, inner knowing, or impressions?
Forrest Messenger: They spoke to me and there was an inner knowing that occurred simultaneous to their communication; it was like revelation that comes through Bible study and prayer.

Rita Bennett: Why were you surprised to see the Tunnel into Heaven picture on Anita Zinter's wall?
Forrest Messenger: Because I have never considered depicting what I saw and the painting on her wall looked so much like what I saw, I was greatly surprised.

Rita Bennett: What did you say to her when you saw what the picture was?
Forrest Messenger: I told her that it looked like what I saw when I had my NDE and then told her my story.

Rita Bennett: What is your walk with Christ like today?
Forrest Messenger: I talk to Him and hear from Him all day. During the week, I have one to one and a-half hours of quiet time and prayer to start my day.

Rita Bennett: How has God blessed you?
Forrest Messenger: I never would have believed I could be redeemed from the bad direction my life was heading prior

to accepting Him into my life. I was very afraid for my future prior to going into high school and could not visualize what I had to hope for. I didn't understand there was a purpose for my life bigger than self-gratification and I did not have any real friends. Today I have many friends, a wonderful wife of twenty-seven years. We have a 15-year-old son who's saved and active in church, and knows God for himself. I have a successful business as a Certified Public Accountant. I have tithed from the day I got saved and I have never been out of work.

Author's Reflection

In Chapter Two, I gave a list of traits of a Near-Death Experience. Forrest had six of the 10 I listed:

#1. a feeling of being dead,

#2. a sense of peace and painlessness,

#3. a supernatural experience of having left earth for another dimension,

#6. a tunnel experience,

#7. seeing people of light,

#9. experiencing a life review.

It is interesting that he had six out of 10 traits of a personal NDE. Trait number 10 that is "a personality transformation upon return" is a possibility for Forrest but the credit for transformation has to come from His acceptance of Jesus as Lord and Savior.

The greatest witness is that Forrest is no longer lost in a "forest" of disillusionment, brokenness, and emptiness that he told us about. It was very important for him to renounce the occult realm he was involved in before darkness could invade deeper into his life. In his youth, he skated very close to the edge.

As I said earlier, this testimony of Forrest Messenger's came to me through a connection with my long-time friend Anita Zinter. She was quite excited when she called me. Anita had a professional meeting with Mr. Messenger and during that time, he saw the framed, *Tunnel of Light into Heaven* she had received from my office. She told me how the picture had affected Forrest, her CPA, and wanted me to know about it.

Anita knew that I was writing a second book on Heaven, and she felt Forrest's message would be a great addition to the book. I met him and his lovely wife at their church. The next week I confirmed adding his experience of going through the *Tunnel of Light* into Heaven. (To see this picture again, turn to the illustration that precedes chapter five in this book, as well as the Color Illustration Collection before *Book Section Two*.)

If Sally and I had not collaboratively created this picture and Taylor had not colorized it, the picture could not have been on Anita's wall for Forrest to see. In that case, we would not have had this interesting chapter and powerful testimony of God's love and grace.

Forrest Messenger now has a "message" for our young people and certainly for parents as well. It is important to remember that not everyone who has a Near-Death Experience gets a second chance to return to make amends, as Forrest did.

I loved hearing of his blessed assurance. Forrest for several decades now has been walking with His Lord. Since his NDE, and then his born again conversion, he *knows* he has eternal life and that he is on the way to Heaven. Looks to me like he will be taking many others with him.

Chapter Eleven's Commentary
Redeemer, Great High Priest, King

Rita Bennett

This picture of Jesus Christ at the beginning of this chapter is a symbolic one, as through it we discover many of His callings. The crown of gold and gems reminds us that His Kingdom will come to earth fully. The High Priest's garments remind us that He is interceding for us now. The prayer shawl *(Tallit)* reminds us of His earthly prayer life and life in a Jewish family in Israel. The wounds in Messiah's hands proclaim He died for a sinful race and yet loves us unconditionally.

Let's look at each of these features.

The Redeemer, Jesus Christ

Because planet Earth was turned over to Satan, the Original Identity Thief, who deceived the first human couple, the darkness of sin, sickness, death, infidelity, murder, and rape invaded the earth. This is called the Fall of Mankind, and even the animals are affected.

Due to our first parents selling out humankind's birthright and the earth's, we have been held hostage by the dark spirit-being, Satan, who is like a combined Stalin, Mussolini, and Hitler rolled into one. This evil one was given, by Adam and Eve's disobedience to God, the title deed to the earth and all in it.

What is the answer to this dilemma which history bears witness to? Someone who had no darkness or evil in him would have to pay the price with his life to buy back, redeem, all that was lost. It was a real battle with a ruthless enemy whose ultimate plan was to usurp the Throne of God.

The End of the Story is told in the fifth chapter of Revelation. Here John says:

And I saw in the right hand of Him who sat on the throne a scroll written inside and on the back, sealed with seven seals. Then I saw a strong angel proclaiming with a loud voice, "Who is worthy to open the scroll and to loose its seals?" And no one in heaven or on the earth was able to open the scroll, or to look at it. So I wept much, because no one was found worthy to open and read the scroll, or to look at it.

But one of the elders said to me, "Do not weep. Behold, the Lion of the tribe of Judah, the Root of David, has prevailed to open the scroll and to loose its seven seals." And I looked, and behold, in the midst of the throne and of the four living creatures, and in the midst of the elders, stood a Lamb as though it had been slain ... Then He [the Lamb] came and took the scroll out of the right hand of Him who sat on the throne.
(Revelation 5:1-7)

Then a song began in Heaven with the Cherubim and the twenty-four elders singing before the Lamb:
You are worthy to take the scroll,
And to open its seals;
For You were slain;
And have redeemed us to God
By Your blood....
(Revelation 5:9a)

Jesus the Christ is the Lamb. His cruel death on the Cross broke the spell—the curse—off the human race. The title deed for the earth and humankind is now once again in the hands and care of our Lord.

But the battle still goes on a little longer. Though Satan was defeated at the Cross when Jesus' blood was poured out, the Enemy won't give up. He still wants to build up his kingdom.

Human beings now have the way to break allegiance with the kingdom of darkness and join the Kingdom of Light. That is, by renouncing Satan, and by saying "Yes" to the Lord Jesus Christ and receiving Him as the great Redeemer. Colossians 1:13 says, "*Who has delivered us from the power of darkness, and has translated us into the Kingdom of Light*" (KJV, mod.).

The earth only has light where people have chosen God's Kingdom of Light. One day, the Day of Grace will be over and the door of the Ark of God will be closed. That has not happened yet. Even when the Heavenly trumpet sounds there will be time but it will be more challenging.

To say "Yes," you can pray John 3:16—the heart of the Bible. Just personalize it and put in your name.

For God so loved the world (and me) that He gave His only begotten Son (for me), that whosoever (that includes me) believes in Him (my Redeemer Jesus) shall not perish but have everlasting life (I receive eternal life right now, and forever). Amen. (It is done.)

Your name has been written in the Lamb's Book of Life. Write the date of this awesome, life transforming new birth in your Bible next to John 3:16. Be sure to share the Good News with someone soon.

The Great High Priest

High Priest's Ephod: Jesus fulfills the role of not only the earthly High Priest, but is now the Great High Priest in Heaven interceding for us. (See Hebrews 7:25.) He carries our names on His shoulders and over His heart in prayer.

Jesus' white linen garment is covered by the shorter blue Ephod which is the Sacred Vestment worn by the High Priest. Samuel and David wore the Ephod on earth. At the bottom of the Ephod were embroidered pomegranates and gold bells, in alternating sequence (see Leviticus 16:4, Exodus 28:33, 34). Dennis and I, in our book *The Holy Spirit and You,* tell how these can symbolically represent the nine fruit (pomegranates) *"love, joy, peace ... "* (Galatians 5:22,23) and the nine spiritual gifts (gold bells) ... *"To one is given the word of wisdom through the Spirit, to another the word of knowledge through the same Spirit ... "* (I Corinthians 12:7-11).

The High Priest's breastplate was worn over his heart. The first High Priest in the Old Testament was Aaron, Moses' brother. We know from the biblical description what a high priest wears. The breastplate had twelve kinds of precious stones representing the twelve tribes of Israel who were shielded from judgment as the High Priest went before God once a year on their behalf during the Day of Atonement.

These precious and semi-precious stones very closely resemble the twelve jewels at the foundation of the walls around Heaven. (See Exodus 28:17-20.) He wore, on each shoulder, an onyx stone with the names of six of the Sons of Israel engraved on each. Since we are now grafted into Israel by our faith, we can see ourselves there spiritually.

Tallit with Star of David

Here you can see Jesus, along with His crown and flowing garment, is wearing a prayer shawl or *tallit.* The Bible does not say Jesus is wearing a prayer shawl in Heaven. Yet, since He is from the tribe of Judah, died a Jew and rose from the dead in a glorified body, it seemed appropriate to have Him wear it in His picture. He still has a Jewish body though it is now no longer subject to physical death. His glorified body can walk through walls, does not need to eat three squares but can eat for enjoyment, and is not confined to time or space (Luke 24:36-43, John 20:25).

Malachi said, *"But unto you that fear my name shall the Sun of righteousness arise with healing in His wings."* This verse is possibly referring to the Jewish prayer shawl that looks similar to wings when. (See Malachi 4:2; Matthew 23:37.)

Obviously, Jesus is not an angel so He does not and never did have wings, though one could also assume in this verse Malachi is speaking figuratively.

Glorious Crown for the King

On earth Jesus was forced to wear a crown of thorns, but at His coronation in Heaven, He will receive a glorious crown because He is the *"King of Kings and Lord of Lords."* Saint John says, *"On His head were many crowns"* (Mark 15:17, Revelation 19:12). We chose the golden crown for Christ, though we realize that Aaron the high priest would have worn a miter of fine linen with a gold plate over the forehead saying "Holiness to the Lord."

Jesus' Wounds of Love

Here it seems our Lord Jesus is telling us and showing us the eternal wounds in the palms of His hands. They reveal how He died by the most cruel form of crucifixion. Jesus Christ chose to give His life for us; in fact, Scripture shows that was the reason He allowed Himself to be born. He willingly laid down His life for us. His nail-scarred hands will always remind us of His everlasting love.

In Heaven, there is preparation for the Marriage Supper of the Lamb going on. Wedding invitations are being sent out. We male and female, His betrothed bride on earth will one day enter into our completed marriage covenant with the Son of God.

John writes, *"Let us be glad and rejoice and give Him glory, for the marriage of the Lamb has come, and His wife has made herself ready"* (Revelation 19:7).

Heaven Tours
Picture Collection

Cherubim Worship God

Tunnel of Light Into Heaven

Redeemer, Great High Priest, King

Arrival at the Eastern Gate

Flight Home to the Heavenly City

Coded Message at the Gate

Map of the New Jerusalem

The Majestic Throne of God

PART TWO

Jesus' Latest Words From Heaven

The Gold Lampstand

G od instructs Moses on Mt. Sinai, "You shall also make a lampstand of pure gold; the lampstand shall be of hammered work. Its shaft, its branches, its bowls, its ornamental knobs, and flowers shall be of one piece (Exodus 25:31,32).

The Lampstand or Menorah, a Judeo-Christian symbol, represents many important constructs: the early Church in Asia, the Church today, the Holy Spirit, the Word of God, the Nation of Israel, the Temple of Israel, the Seven-fold Spirit of God, Judaism, the Lord Jesus who walks among the lamps, the Five Wise Virgins who had oil, the last days Church, and the Holy Place in the Temple.

155

The Seven Churches and You

One might wonder while reading the following chapters, whether the three first chapters of Revelation were written exclusively for "the Church." If so, one might ask, "Who then is the Church and does that include me?" I will answer that for you.

The translators of the New Testament chose to use words that in the first century would not have been coined yet. Jesus himself did not call the people gathered—church, or a building for worship—the Church. This noun was added to the believer's vocabulary later.

Jewish people then, and today, would instead speak of their people as a community, or congregation. The Greek word *synagogue* means a gathering of people, a congregation, a place of prayer (Acts 16:13).

A Jewish congregation today that has accepted Jesus as Messiah is called a "Messianic Community or Congregation." In fact, Dr. Stern's name for the Seven Churches is "Seven Messianic Communities" (Stern, *Complete Jewish Bible*, 1998, The Revelation, 1:4, p.1533,1605).

Jesus spoke Hebrew to the Jewish people and read in Hebrew, the Torah, Isaiah, and Psalms in the Synagogue. Hebrew Scriptures were not only read but sung. Hebrew was Jesus' *(Yeshua's)* first language from childhood.

It is believed by Greek scholars such as William F. Dankenbring, that Jesus also spoke Greek and Aramaic since He spent some of his formative years in Galilee, 90 miles north of Jerusalem.

The first believers in Jesus as Messiah were known as *The Way, or Disciples of Jesus* (Acts 9:2). The Apostles were known as "the twelve." The early believers were first of all Jews, as Jesus came for His own chosen race first, then also for the Greeks. Paul says, "For I am not ashamed of the gospel of Christ, for it is the power of God to salvation for everyone who believes, for the Jew first and also for the Greek" (Romans 1:16).

The Greeks were also in God's plan to be used as translators of the Bible from Hebrew and Aramaic into Greek.

Jesus however did not leave out the Gentiles (the nations). He chose the Jewish scholar, Saul, whom He renamed Paul, to become a Messianic apostle to the Gentiles.

Jesus, in essence, ordained Saul in absentia when a bright light shone around Paul and he fell down under the power of the Spirit—while on the road to Damascus to persecute Believers of "The Way" (Acts 9:3-6). The Lord spoke to Saul from Heaven saying:

"Saul, Saul why are you persecuting Me?"

And he said, "Who are You, Lord?"

Then the Lord said, "I am Jesus, whom you are persecuting. It is hard for you to kick against the goads."

[A goad is a pointed stick for urging stubborn oxen.]

Next Saul asked a great question that we would be wise to ask:

So he trembling and astonished, said, "Lord, what do You want me to do?"

Then the Lord said to him, "Arise and go into the city, and you will be told what to do." (Acts 9:4-6).

Saul had been blinded by the light of God. Having been led to Damascus, he lay on a bed in darkness and on a total fast for three days. Meanwhile God spoke to the strong believer, Ananias, and told him to go to Saul "the persecutor of believers" and pray for his physical healing, pray for his filling with the Spirit, and to baptize him.

Paul's blind eyes were healed "within an hour" of the laying-on-of hands, he was filled to overflowing with the Spirit, and baptized. (Acts 9: 17, 18) For the next three years, Paul prepared himself to become a spiritual leader to do the work of an empowered apostle, teacher, and evangelist.

Paul soon realized that his call was to the Gentiles. *"Behold we turn to the Gentiles. 'For so the Lord has commanded us: I have set you as a light to the Gentiles that you should be for salvation to the ends of the earth'"* (Acts 13:46-48).

To them, and to all others who would believe in the Messiah Jesus, the Apostle Paul wrote two-thirds of the New Testament (Wiki Answers; Answers.com, 2008). Our Lord did not leave out non-Jewish believers. He loves us all, whatever our background, color, or language may be.

So who is a member of the Church? Basically it is anyone who has believed in, and continues to believe in, the Lord Jesus Christ as Savior and Lord.

"Church comes from the Greek *ekklesia*, 'called out.' The church is employed to express various ideas, some of which are scriptural, others not. It may be used to signify: (1) The entire body of those who are saved by their relation to Christ. (2) A particular Christian denomination. (3) The aggregate of all the ecclesiastical communions professing faith in Christ ..." (Unger, 1985, p. 236).

Some Do Not Like the Term

If after reading my treatise, you still do not like the term "Church" then substitute a more likeable biblical term.

I cannot tell you how many times at my secular university I've had a student say to me, "I used to be a member of the Church, but now I am a (fill in the blank)." "I used to be a Christian, but now I am a (again fill in the blank)."

Though I was careful not to push my faith on anyone, somehow "Christian" must have been written on my face or discerned in my voice. One student, with no provocation on my part, said, chiding me in class, "You are a little 'Church' girl."

Though I learned many lessons in the Halls of Ivy, it was good to graduate and not have to be so extra careful. It did let me know, however, that today the Church is not admired as much as I had once thought. Or has it always been this way?

Jesus is not a "Christian"

A popular fiction book came out where the dialogue has Jesus emphatically stating, "I'm not a Christian." Actually the book should have had Jesus saying, "*Inee lo notsree.*"

But of course Jesus would not have used the term "Christian," or "*notsree*" in Hebrew (as I transliterated it), since the title of Christian had not yet been coined. Secondly, He would not have been narcissistically calling "himself a follower of himself!"

"Christian" is *Christianos* in Greek. The disciples were formally called Christians first in Antioch (see Acts 11:26)" (Tenny Ed., 1963-1971, p. 162). That means the official date for this new name for believers was in 41 A.D. Jesus was not living on earth when "Christian" came into use, as He'd died, rose again and returned Home a decade before.

Jesus' birth was about 4 B.C. and so His death at age 33 was likely in the year 29 or 30 A.D. Fortunately at that time He also experienced resurrection and forty days later ascension—never to die again. Our Gregorian calendar was established in 1582, hundreds of years after

Christ's birth. Consequently, without precise methods of dating, it was set four or five years too late concerning the use of B.C. and A.D.

"To the first Christians, their own name mattered not at all: their concern was with the one Name of Jesus Christ (Acts 3:16).

"Inevitably, the name which they invoked was given to them: Christians, Christ's men [or women]" (Ibid. Tenny, p.162).

Lately, I've had my fill of hearing religious and non-religious souls putting down the terms Church, Christian, and Christianity. As the Rev. Canon Dennis Bennett, my late husband and world-renowned Charismatic leader, used to warn naysayers, "Do not kick down the ladder you climbed up on."

Remember that the early Christians did not have the New Testament as we have today since the Gospels and Epistles were just being written! And only the most educated could read and write. They were mainly reading, or more likely hearing read, the Scrolls or the Parchments of the Old Testament.

In 70 A.D., the majestic Herodian Second Temple and City of Jerusalem were burned by the future Roman Emperor Titus. It was the first Roman-Jewish War. Next, the war at Mount *Masadah* took place as the last stronghold of Judean patriots held out against Roman rule for the next three years, A.D. 71-73. "The prolonged Roman siege ended in mass suicide by the rebels to avoid captivity" (Baltsan, 1991, p. 241).

Jews who escaped extermination during those years were forbidden to live in Jerusalem or to speak Hebrew conversationally. "During the second century, the center of Jewish life shifted to Galilee, a region in which the mixed population spoke Aramaic and Greek" (Rothblum, Bergman and Band, 1987, p. vi).

The exception was that the rabbis were allowed to continue to read the Hebrew scrolls in the Synagogues. Biblical Hebrew would never be lost, but Hebrew as a spoken language would eventually become a dead language for 1700 years.

Miraculously, before the founding of the State of Israel, a Russian Editor with a divine mission, Eliezer Ben-Yehuda, moved to Jerusalem and with much hard labor and sacrifice became known as "the father of spoken Hebrew." When he died in 1922, he had completed sixteen Volumes of the *Dictionary of Ancient and Modern Hebrew* (Stachorek, 2008, www.Israelmybeloved.com).

As a Judeo-Christian I am interested in my Jewish roots as well as my Christian ones. I invite you to read on as I, with great care, attempt to decipher the messages Jesus Christ left for what is called today the seven "Churches of Revelation."

Of course, Jesus was *not* a "Christian," but He *is* the "Christ" in the name Christian. Our Lord is not against Christians or the Church, imperfect though we may be. He loves us enough to help us glean from these seven ancient letters, messages that we need to know in the challenging times in which we live.

The "Churches" throughout these two millennia represent all believing people, so in this second part of *Heaven Tours* please consider the term *inclusive* rather than *exclusive*.

God has left a message for you, personally. Let it change your life.

CHAPTER THIRTEEN

People Want to Know About Heaven

Not long ago I was visiting with an Edmonds businesswoman I had not seen for some months. She told me about attending a Women's Faith-based Convention where in small breakout groups they studied the Book of Revelation.

My friend, Jamie, had gone to church for years but had not had teaching on this particular book.

As we've already found, Revelation has a lot to say about Heaven. It's written by one of the four gospel writers, the Apostle John.

The women took turns sharing their perceptions about Heaven and how they were looking forward to it. Then Jamie's turn came up.

She said something like, "I cannot get too excited about leaving earth since I have so many things to do with my life, family, and work. And what Heaven is like is still a mystery to me."

One member of the group responded that she thought Jamie seemed complacent about a believer's future home! Jamie left that night rather annoyed with the woman and tried to forgive her confrontational attitude.

The second Bible study took them further into the first three books of Revelation.

Here it shows a picture of the Seven Churches of Asia Minor that have been seen first to represent all the churches named, as well as subsequent generations including ours today.

Seven is the biblical number of completeness. An angel showed the Apostle John the seven churches in the form of a seven-branch candlestick or more biblically correct a lampstand. These oil lamps, biblical scholars believe, are based on the Jewish Temple lampstand (*menorah*).

The Lord gave Moses the design for the original seven-lamp menorah in the Books of Moses (Exodus 25:31-40). Concerning the lampstand, "The first century Jewish historian, Flavius Josephus confirms, 'It was made with its knops, and lilies, and pomegranates, and bowls (which ornaments amounted to seventy in all)'" (Somerville, 2008, p. 6).

Jamie says she became excited when she saw how God had given a personal message to each church.

In my own review of the chapters, I saw that Jesus first gave a message of *affirmation* (a good way to begin a confrontation); secondly, He gave each a detailed *warning* about their behavior; following this He challenged each to *repent*—make an about face. Then the Lord described the *reward* that each will receive if that church lives as an "overcomer."

Affirm, warn, repent, and reward—four good steps for us from the greatest Teacher of all. Two out of the seven churches did not have our Lord's criticism and they are the *churches of Smyrna*, and *Philadelphia*.

The angel gave John this special vision into Heaven. It begins when John hears a loud voice, as of a trumpet, saying:

"I am the Alpha and the Omega, the First and the Last," and *"What you see, write in a book and send it to the seven churches which are in Asia: to Ephesus, to Smyrna, to Pergamos, to Thyatira, to Sardis, to Philadelphia, and to Laodicea."*

John sees Jesus:

"Then I turned to see the voice that spoke with me. And having turned I saw seven golden lampstands and in the midst of the seven lampstands One like unto the Son of Man, clothed with a garment down to the feet, and girded about the chest with a golden band.... And His countenance was like the sun shining in His strength." (Revelation 1:11-13, 16b)

So Jesus is in the center or the light in the midst of the seven Churches or lampstands. He is walking around, and from Heaven's viewpoint, observing how they are doing. This gets exciting, doesn't it?

It did for Jamie too. After learning about these beginning chapters, she said she's much, more enthusiastic about Heaven! I'm happy to report, also, that the two women were fully reconciled.

I Needed to Study these Messages from Jesus

I, too, have needed to study these last messages of Jesus, as it's rarely been taught in my experience. Perhaps it has not been the right time for it until now. In chapters two and three, Jesus' Words are not coming from earth but rather coming directly from Heaven. The beloved Disciple, the Apostle John, was the chosen conduit for these Words to flow to us from Heaven to earth. He was a literal pipeline from Heaven.

In these beginning chapters, you will see a word picture of the Seven Churches of Asia Minor from first-century times. The messages were first sent to all the churches named above. Interestingly these cities were built close to one another and on a major Roman postal route. The rider could make a geographical semi-circular route beginning southwest from Ephesus traveling north, then east, and south east—just as the cities are listed in biblical order. (Adapted from: *The Spirit-Filled Life Bible*, p. 1960).

Many Bible scholars believe the prophetic messages were given not only for the early church two-thousand years ago, but for subsequent generations including ours in the twenty-first century. I hope that we can learn some important things to help us become better witnesses in the world, and to become more pleasing to our Lord.

If God has left a message for His believers today, it seems we should try to decipher it. It's good to study these biblical messages to see if we are measuring up. Even the daily news often points out that it is past time for believers to do this.

Let's see what we can discover to help us in the next seven chapters.

CHAPTER FOURTEEN

God Loves You, So Repent Already

The Church of Ephesus

The small Greek Island of Patmos, then a Roman penal colony, is where the last living apostle, John, was banished by one of the Roman emperors. The crime was John's faithful witness *"for the Word of God and for the testimony of Jesus Christ"* (Revelation 1:9). Though it was far from a "vacation holiday" for John, even though surrounded by the beautiful Aegean Sea, with God's strength and no doubt with tremendous struggles he wrote down the prophetic messages to the seven churches.

The sea separated the seven churches to the north of the Apostle John while he was incarcerated on the Isle of Patmos. Patmos itself was ten miles by six miles and located sixty miles southwest of Ephesus. Today this province of Asia is known as the coast of Turkey.

First on the list for God to speak to is the church at Ephesus. The time of this church's existence is approximately 30 to 33 A.D., that is the birth of the Church at Pentecost, until about 98 A.D. when the Apostle John died.

Paul was martyred 67 A.D., Timothy was martyred 72 A.D., and John died in 98 A.D. The precious leaders of the Church were gone. "The lampstand has gone from its place." By the middle of the second century, settlers of Asiatic origin were main inhabitants (Tenny, 1963, p. 254).

Revelation of Jesus Christ

In John's vision, he saw in Jesus' right hand seven stars or angels and we find that this is referring to the seven leaders of those churches.

"To the angel of the church of Ephesus write, These things says He who holds the seven stars in His right hand, who walks in the midst of the seven golden lampstands" (Rev. 2:1).

- Holds the seven stars in right hand
- Walks in the midst of seven golden lampstands

The angel or bishop at this time was most probably Timothy, who presided over that church before St. John took up his final residence there. Timothy is supposed to have continued in that office until 97 A.D. and to have been martyred a short time before St. John's return from Patmos (Clarke, 1801, vol. V, p. 975).

The Apostle Paul also lived at Ephesus three years as a missionary and to them he later, while in a Roman prison, wrote the Epistle to the Ephesians (Acts 20:31). The "mystery" of God's plan for the Church is revealed in Ephesians as in no other Epistle. Many Believers, including myself, have benefited from chapter six, which teaches what we call today, *The Whole Armor of God.*

Affirmation

Christ's affirmation to the church at Ephesus:

"I know your works, and your labor, your patience, and you cannot bear those who are evil. And you have

tested those who say they are apostles and are not, and found them liars; and you have persevered and have patience, and have labored for My name's sake and have not become weary. " (Revelation 2:2,3)

- Know your works, labor, and patience
- You cannot bear those who are evil
- Tested those who "claim" to be apostles
- Have not become weary and labored for Me

It was not easy to be a Christian in the early days of the Church. (At times it's not easy for us now.) Here Jesus is concerned about His small infant Church's survival. He is coaching them on how to survive the battle with the "world, the flesh and the Devil." Everything He says may not fit exactly what is happening to us today but some of it is familiar.

False Apostles

First of all, originally there were twelve official apostles entrusted with the work of Christ who is, "the Apostle and High Priest of our confession" (Hebrews 4:14-16).

The apostles names are given in the illustration in Chapter 7, *"The Coded Message at the Gates."* At the twelve Gates of the entrances to Heaven, you may remember seeing their names written at the base of each doorway: "Peter, Andrew, James, John, Philip, Bartholomew, James—the Little, Judas— Thaddaeus, Simon Zelotes, Matthew, Thomas, and Matthias.

These twelve—eleven of whom were martyred and one incarcerated for decades—will be honored eternally due to their faithfulness. (Recommended resource: Foxe, John, *Foxe's Book of Martyrs.*)

The apostles, who at the beginning were disciples, walked with Jesus as He headed for the ultimate beachhead landing of the Kingdom of God on Planet Earth. When the Gospel flag of faith was planted in Jerusalem, one giant God-step was taken for humanity.

An apostle is "one sent with a special message or commission." The original qualification of an apostle, as stated by Peter (Acts 1:21-22), is that he should have been personally acquainted with our Lord's ministry from His baptism by John to His ascension. By this close personal relation with Him, they were peculiarly fitted to give testimony to the facts of redemption. Shortly after their redemption, "*He gave to them authority over unclean spirits, to cast them out, and to heal every kind of disease and every kind of sickness; and sent them out in pairs' to preach*" (Matthew 10:1-6; Mark 3:14, 16:17; Luke 6:1,13; 9:1) (Unger, 1957/88, p. 87).

Paul was not one of the twelve, but he declared *himself "an apostle, not sent from men, nor through the agency of man"* (Galatains1:1), and commissioned directly from Christ when he had a visionary encounter with Him on the Road to Damascus. (See Acts 9:3-19.) Some call him the thirteenth apostle.

There are battles about who is considered a legitimate apostle today. There are historic churches coming down from the early apostles. Many debates there are as to which church came first. Then there are non-historic churches that are of the belief that God has called them as apostles, or in an apostolic ministry of founding churches for their denomination. Of course, God is the ultimate judge for such titles.

But in the church at Ephesus Jesus was aware of wolves that had gotten into the flock, and the leaders apparently had this discernment also. When false prophets invade the flock, many in the church fall away. This is not a lot of fun. As a pastor's wife for twenty-five years, I saw how the gift of discernment was given to protect the flock through my late husband, the Reverend Dennis Joseph Bennett.

The church at Ephesus began in the purity of bride to the Bridegroom. In these writings, we see how Christ longs for that close relationship with His Church that He had at the beginning.

Repent

Jesus' Correction:

"*Nevertheless I have this against you, that you have left your first love. Remember from where you have fallen; repent and do the first works, or else I will come to you quickly and remove your lampstand from its place—unless you repent.*" (Revelation 2:4, 5)

Here is an allusion to the seven candlestick [menorah] in the tabernacle and temple, which could not be removed without suspending the whole Levitical service. So the threatening here intimates that, if they did not repent, he would unchurch them; they should no longer have a pastor, no longer have the word and sacraments, and no longer have the presence of the Lord Jesus (Ibid. Clarke, p. 976).

For the unrepentant individual, candlestick or lampstand removal could mean a shortened life, or diminished place of leadership, or worst of all—the eternal consequences of apostasy.

When I thought about the church at Ephesus and the correction the Lord had for her, it at first seemed curious to me. I reasoned that they must have done well for many years. Paul, Timothy, and John had taught them! They had the best teachers possible. What happened?

I Was Losing My First Love

Then I remembered my own early twenties when in college in Florida. I was a Sunday go-to-church believer most of the time, when I did go I was not being fed spiritually. During my college years, I was slowly falling away from the centrality of my childhood faith.

171

After graduation, I was invited to a home where people gathered together to have Bible Study and to pray. A close friend of mine who attended this group had just died.

The leader asked if I would like to have prayer. I agreed to the invitation. Several people gathered round me to join in. All of a sudden, I began to weep many tears of sadness about how I had often ignored my "first love"—Jesus.

I could have been embarrassed but the tears felt so good and cleansing. All I can say is that my life has never been the same since that day.

I mourned and repented for my sins, and I mourned the death of my friend, Gail. Jesus said in the Beatitudes, *"Blessed are those who mourn for they shall be comforted"* (Matthew 5:4). I believe mourning is a gift and a blessing. Truly, I was comforted and Jesus has remained my forever-best Friend. Jesus is near—He is "at hand" for you also.

It's About Love

The Holy Spirit recently reminded me that "it's about Love." It is the importance of love first of all, for Jesus and our romance as His Bride, His help-mate—male and female. The Greek word for love in this verse in Revelation is the highest form—"*agape*[14] self-sacrificial love, affection, dear love" (Strong, 1984, #26, p. 7). He gave His all for us. What will we give in return? Then too, it is God's love that spills over to everyone we come in contact with.

I am reminded of 1 Corinthians 13, the greatest chapter on love. This chapter written by the Apostle Paul ends with powerful words: *"The greatest of these is love."* We learned this early in our faith walk. Remember?

What then could keep the early Ephesians out of Heaven as some biblical teachers feel could have happened to the unrepentant? I'm sure Heaven is the most loving place in all universes. We are not going to Heaven to learn how to love Jesus and others, are we? The "Boot Camp for Love" to prepare us for Heaven begins down here on earth. When we get to the Kingdom, we will be exhibiting the fruit of love. No one is going to Heaven shouting angry words at the angel standing at the gate, are they? So anger has to be dealt with down here.

A true agape love relationship with God will not diminish but grow. There is no effect of the "second law of thermodynamics" as there is on earth, "When given enough time ... relationships, marriages, will cool down."

Something was wrong at the heart with many in the church in Ephesus. The Lord's instructions were to do the first works of their faith. They had moved away from the basic foundation. God had to shock them by speaking, shouting, as a Heavenly trumpet to them.

Why weren't they witnessing to anyone like they used to? Why were they shortening prayer time or not teaching others about the Books of Moses and some of the New Testament Scrolls? Did they forget the importance of fasting and praying when they realized they were falling out of love with God?

The great commandment Jesus said is, *"You shall love the LORD your God with all your heart, with all your soul, and with all your mind." The second is like it: "You shall love your neighbor as yourself"* (Matthew 22:37-39).

I believe Jesus our Messiah was calling the Ephesians then, and us today, back to love.

What Treasures we Have

In comparison to those early millennia, we in North America have so many more opportunities to develop our relationship with God. Taking a quick count, I'm looking at ten Bible translations, and five Bible commentaries, and several Greek and Hebrew Lexicons in my little office.

Also I have a computer that through Google can take me to any Bible I want to read and in as many languages as I want. I recently discovered this particular computer help. The

Ephesians would have been blown away to consider having such treasures. Everything had to be written by hand back then.

Some experiences that helped my love for God stay kindled were taking three trips to Israel, and over ten years studying the Hebrew language that Jesus spoke in the Synagogue. *Inee metabarret evret kesot,* the transliteration means, "I speak a little Hebrew."

Sharing in *The Edmonds Beacon* newspaper and my *Worship Column* has opened many wonderful discussions with people in my hometown of Edmonds, Washington. Sharing my faith gives me joy.

One of Jesus' announcements was, *"Repent, for the kingdom of heaven is at hand"* (Matthew 4:17). The good news is that the Kingdom of God is still "at hand" even though Jesus the Christ is no longer physically on earth. "At hand" means Christ's presence is always available to you. All you and I need to do is call Him. Jeremiah 33:3 is like God's telephone number. Look it up.

Affirmation

Second Affirmation from the Lord: *"But this you have, that you hate the deeds of the Nicolaitans, which I also hate"* (2:6).

Here Jesus affirms the Ephesians for something good right after He has corrected and warned them strongly about their lifestyle. This encourages them, and us, with the knowledge that God has not given up on the Ephesians nor has He given up on us.

Some good things have been going on in the Church. However, we cannot miss the vital step of repentance as we too have been strongly warned.

There are some things God hates: The Greek meaning for Nicolaitans means "to conquer the laity." (*"Nikos, nee'kos;* conquest, triumph," *Strong's* 3534). "The Church elders are supposed to be shepherds and examples to the flock, not those who suppress the laity. The Apostle Peter says, *"... Not as being lords over those entrusted to you, but being examples to the flock"* (1 Peter 5:3).

Sometimes the Church hierarchy today can work as a pyramid where the average members at the bottom are rarely heard from and their gifts not acknowledged. It is important to offer opportunities and encouragement for all members to grow and develop. After all, the Church is called to be a light to the world. If suppressed, their light, their Menorah, will be quenched.

Heresies: Nicolaitans, Gnosticism, Balaam Abuse

Nicolaitans are a group of persons whose works both the church at Ephesus and our Lord hated (Revelation 2:6) and whose doctrine was held by some in the Pergamene church (Revelation 2:15). Their doctrine was similar to that of Balaam through whose influence the Israelites ate things sacrificed to idols and committed fornication. A sect of Nicolaitans existed among the Gnostics in the third century, as is known from church fathers of the time. It [Nicolaitan belief] probably had its origin in the group condemned in Revelation. (Ibid., Tenny, p. 586).

"The first century Church was engaged in a huge battle with Gnosticism, which basically taught that it did not really matter what the body did, as long the spirit/mind was saved. In other words, it doesn't matter how I live as long as I believe the right stuff ... Suffice it to say that Jesus hates any doctrine that says holiness and obedience to the commands of God are optional" (www.truthablaze.com/ephesus.html, 9-3-08).

Temptations

Here are the biggest temptations to the Ephesians. Diana was hailed as the great goddess of the Ephesians who was worshipped by the city, in the Temple of Diana (Acts 19:34-35). ("*Artemis.* One of the Greek goddesses, a huntress. The

Roman name and KJV rendering is Diana." Unger, *Merrill, Bible Dictionary*, p.110.)

This was breaking, the second Commandment—that of Idolatry. Idolatry is often coupled with Fornication or Adultery, that of breaking the seventh Commandment. This joined with the Nicolaitans and Gnostics encouraging sexual sins was not easy to resist even by some in the first century Church of "The Way."

No matter what temptations there are around us, God still calls us to a life of holiness, repentance, and sacrifice.

Reward

Jesus offers a reward to the repentant, *"He who has an ear, let him hear what the Spirit says to the churches. To him who overcomes will I give to eat of the tree of life, which is in the midst of the Paradise of God"* (Revelation 2:7).

Eat from the Tree of Life in Paradise

What a gift this is! We know at the beginning after God created the Garden of Eden and the first man and woman, they had an enormous test. God said to Adam that all the fruit trees were there to be enjoyed, even the Tree of Life, but from the Tree of the Knowledge of Good and Evil they were not to eat or they would die. Then the "Tempting Con-Artist" of the universe, Satan, possessed a snake so he could talk to the first married couple.

He tempted Eve first as he knew Adam would follow her. Eve was convinced that eating the fragrant, beautiful fruit would cause her to be as God and very wise. She ate and then passed it on to Adam. They died spiritually, became alienated from God, and hid from Him.

God had to remove them from the Garden so that they would not eat from the Tree of Life and live forever in this condition. They lost their sexual innocence, they had to toil over the land, childbirth would be dangerous and excruciatingly painful, the first murder would occur, and sickness and death would be the norm. Unknown to them at that time was the depth of what they had done. They had lost their birthright dominion of the world, handing it over to Satan on a silver platter.

Now prior to this, the angel Lucifer (renamed Satan) had started a rebellion in Heaven to take over God's throne and had consequently been tossed out of Heaven to live in the second heaven of outer space. That day in the Garden he had invaded earth and brought his kingdom of darkness to the earth. One third of the angels—now known as demons—had fallen with him.

God could have wiped out the entire human race for their sin and decided to start over. Fortunately for us God had fallen in love with us—His creation—and chose to save us. Therefore, the Triune God *Yahweh*: Father, Son, and Holy Spirit had a meeting and set up a plan to redeem humankind. It required the death of God's Son, Jesus Christ, to take away our sins by dying in our place. Because of Christ's great sacrifice for us, we had a way of escape from becoming spiritual prisoners of Satan eternally.

That's in brief the story of the Bible. It's about God's plan to rescue us. It starts in Genesis 2:7 and ends in Revelation 22:2. After Jesus died and rose from the dead, the power of Satan was broken forever for those who choose to accept God's redeeming love.

Jesus is the One who saved the human race but in order to actually have eternal life, symbolized in the Tree of Life, we individually must choose to leave darkness and be born into God's family and Kingdom of Light.

To the Ephesians, and to us, Jesus urges us by faith to eat from the Tree of Life and live forever. This gift is free, yet it is worth more than anyone could ever pay.

You can be an overcomer by trusting in Jesus, the Lamb of God, who takes away the sin of the world; by sharing the word of your testimony of salvation and empowerment; and by being willing to give your life to and for Him. (See Revelation 12:11.)

Yes, in Heaven we will be eating from the literal Trees of Life that produce twelve kinds of divine fruit. Even the leaves of the trees will be healing for the nations, for all people. (See Revelation 22:2.)

A Moment to Reflect and Pray:

Take a moment to relax and think about all our Lord has said to you in this chapter. His words from Heaven have come down to warn you, to protect you, and to love you. God has fallen in love with you and wants to live close to you. He wants you to talk over life's problems with Him.

Are you lagging behind on your journey with the Good Shepherd? What steps can you take to renew your commitment to your forever, Best Friend and Lover? Remember He passionately wants to be your First Love—now and always.

Take a deep breath and relax in His Perfect Love. If you haven't done it yet, open your heart to Jesus and invite Him in to be your Friend forever. Tell Jesus what is on your heart.

He wants to listen, forgive you, and support you. Repent if you have grown cold and have let the glitter and temptations of the world take His place. Name your sins and offer them up to Him. Only He can truly satisfy.

CHAPTER FIFTEEN

Persecuted but Beloved

The Church of Smyrna

The second church Christ personally addresses in the Book of Revelation is Smyrna, known as the persecuted church. Smyrna has myrrh in its name, an aromatic exudation from a thorny tree, used for holy healing ointment. It well describes a persecuted church. The Three Kings presented gifts to Baby Jesus of: gold, frankincense, and myrrh. The gift of myrrh was prophetic of Jesus' coming death.

Interesting that Smyrna was called "the crown of Ionia—the ornament of Asia. It is now the chief city of SW Turkey, with a population of more than one and one-half million."[15]

Revelation of Jesus Christ

Let's have ears to hear what Jesus says to the church.

"And to the angel (pastor) of the church of Smyrna write: These things says the first and the last, who was dead, and came to life" (Revelation 2:8). What a proclamation of Christ's divinity!

- The first and the last
- Was dead and came to life!

He is the *Alpha* and *Omega*, which is "first and last" translated into Greek. Or the *Aleph* and the *Tav*.

Jesus said, "Do not be afraid; I am the First and the Last. I am He who lives, and was dead, and behold I am alive forevermore. Amen. And I have the keys of Hades and of Death." (Revelation 1:17b-18)

Christ also proclaims His redemptive death and resurrection. These two proclamations were very encouraging for Believers in Smyrna who have been so abused. After all, earth is not giving them much to rejoice about but Christians are taught to look forward to their own resurrection.

Temptation of Leader "Worship"

The city of Smyrna was heavily into Roman emperor worship. It was compulsory for every citizen to openly worship the emperor by burning a pinch of incense to Caesar and calling Caesar "Lord." This was a cult of "self worship" and "self-aggrandizement." The consequence for not obeying this edict was death. The famous martyr, Polycarp, is one of the pastors, who was burned at the stake for refusing to obey this edict. (This happened around 169 A.D.)

To worship the emperor would break God's first Commandment, written with the finger of God on stone at Mount Sinai, *"You shall have no other gods before Me"* (Exodus 20:3).

This situation must have been awful for God's children. They were consistently being tempted to call the emperor "Lord" in order to have food, a job and a home. No other being can be called Lord other than the true and living God!

This was the earliest trick of Satan. Caesar's edict to be worshipped was satanically inspired.

Satan said at the Great Temptation of Jesus, *"If you [Jesus] will worship me, all shall be yours"* (Luke 4:7 KJV, mod.). *"And Jesus answered and said to him, Get behind me, Satan: for it is written, you shall worship the Lord your God, and Him only shall you serve"* (Luke 4:8, mod.). Jesus won this temptation for himself and for you and me.

In May 1996, while on a tour bus, we passed by the Mount of Temptation in the Israeli desert. It was hot and the mountain was barren and very dry. Now I could visualize the battle Jesus had with temptation as He fasted and prayed forty days and nights. He was preparing for one of His greatest battles as He confronted Satan. This battle was won and the last battle was completed once and for all on the Cross. Jesus' great proclamation was, *"It is finished!"* (John 19:30).

"The main work of the Holy Spirit is to bring people under the Lordship of Jesus" (Hayford, *Spirit-Filled Life Bible*, p. 1736). This is the call for all believers to proclaim the Lordship of Jesus Christ and to help others accept Him as Lord.

Affirmation

Jesus finds no fault with Smyrna. He says, *"I know your works, and tribulation, and poverty, (but you are rich)"* (Revelation 2:9a).

- Good works
- Walking through tribulation
- You are rich in God

They did not have earthly riches, but rather, a flourishing heavenly bank account. The Apostle Matthew says, *"Lay up for yourselves treasures in Heaven, where neither moth or rust destroys and where thieves do not break in and steal. For where your treasure is, there your heart will be also"* (Matthew 6:20, 21). How wonderful to live your life so our Lord God will say, "I've found no fault in you."

Warning

"And I hear the lie in the claims of those who pretend to be good Jews, who in fact belong to Satan's crowd" (Revelation

2:9b, *The Message Bible*). Just as Christians should not persecute Jews, Jews should not persecute Christians.

Saul, who became the Apostle Paul, was previously hunting down Christians to imprison them and assisting those who killed them. The first mention of this was in the stoning of Stephen. (See Acts 7:54-60.)

We remember Paul's conversion on the Damascus Road. There Jesus asked Paul (Saul of Tarsus) why he was persecuting Him (Acts 9:4). Paul was persecuting the Church, but Jesus let him know that he was actually persecuting *Him!* Yet, God forgave Paul.

The Church is Christ's body on Earth. Here we see how the Lord in Heaven is strongly defensive about what is done to His Body of Believers.

Reward

Do not fear any of those things which you are about to suffer. Indeed, the devil is about to throw some of you into prison, that you may be tested, and you will have tribulation ten days. Be faithful until death, and I will give you a crown of life. (Revelation 2:10, *The Message Bible*)

A crown of life. Here we see Jesus saying, "The devil will throw some of you in prison." The enemy uses people to accomplish his goals of destruction. The period of "ten days" could mean that they will be in this situation for a short time.

Why doesn't Jesus stop the persecution the Devil is fomenting? To answer this, remember what we've studied showing the fall of man, the death and resurrection of Jesus, and how there is still a real battle between God's Kingdom and Satan's kingdom. This is what has been going on in this beautiful blue planet since the beginning of the human race.

Serious Persecution

As in all wars, we win some and lose some. The news media in 2008 reported about John McCain's five years as Prisoner of War in Viet Nam. At least two times a Christian prison guard risked his life to help John. Once during the night, to loosen the ropes, that were tied around his arms painfully forcing his head between his legs.

A second time, when Mr. McCain was allowed to go outside the toxic prison to breathe fresh air for a few minutes, the guard who was in charge looked in John's eyes and made the sign of the Cross in the sand with his foot—then erased it. What an encouragement to Navy aviator John McCain that he had not been forgotten by God or man.

If you've read the end of the Bible you'll know the war will be won by God's side.

Then *I saw an angel coming down from Heaven, having the key to the bottomless pit and a great chain in his hand. He laid hold of the dragon, that serpent of old, who is the Devil and Satan, and bound him. ...* (Revelation 20:1-2)

Christ tells the Smyrnaites not to be afraid of the suffering and perhaps martyrdom ahead. Yes, there is something better than life on this earth. Even today, there are people all over this planet being persecuted for their faith.

On November the 4, 2005, the *One Jerusalem* newsletter says, "In Indonesia, three teenage Christian girls were beheaded near a church." The terrorists who did this and all other persecutors, unless they repent, will receive God's eternal judgment. I am sure these dear teenage girls have joined with the Smyrna saints and millions of others who were persecuted for their faith while on earth. These teens have received Martyr's Crowns for eternity.

Jesus who was the most persecuted person on earth, challenges us with, *"Pray for them who despitefully use you, and persecute you"* (Matthew 5:44). Oh! That is hard to do! The reason, I think, He tells us this is so we will have less ulcers and wrinkles, and who knows the persecutors might just repent and join the family of God.

Reward

> *He who has an ear, let him hear what the Spirit says to the churches. He who overcomes shall not be hurt by the second death.* (Revelation 2:11)

Not hurt by the second death. I heard a saying about "the second death" years ago. "If you are born twice you will die once; if you are born once you will die twice." Everyone on earth has been born once but Jesus made a strong statement to the Jewish ruler Nicodemus, *"You must be born again"* (John 3:7b).

Those who have been born again, receiving Jesus and His teachings into his or her life, will appear at the judgment (Bema) seat of Christ. The purpose will be to joyfully receive rewards according to what we have done. (See Romans 14:10b.)

Sadly, one group of people will die twice. They were born physically but not spiritually. These who have rejected Christ and His teachings, whose names are not in the Book of Life, will appear at the White Throne Judgment to be sentenced. This is the second death. (See Revelation 20:11-14.)

The name Overcomer is used many times in the seven letters to the churches. Here is a good definition of it by the Apostle John:

> *"For whatever is born of God overcomes the world. And this is the victory that has overcome the world—our faith. Who is he who overcomes the world but he who believes that Jesus is the Son of God?"* (1 John 5:4, 5)

A Moment to Reflect and Pray

Take a moment to relax and think of the Overcomer's life. To be an Overcomer you cannot do it alone. You need faith for victory. *"Faith comes by hearing and hearing by the Word of God"* (Romans 10:17). Faith comes by receiving Jesus, the giver of faith into your life. The supernatural gift of faith comes through empowerment of the Holy Spirit. The fruit of faith comes as you mature in Christ. You have been absorbing faith and strengthening your spirit as you have been reading Jesus' Words from Heaven.

Invite Him into your life as the Son of God and your Lord. Renounce any false gods you may have given allegiance to. If necessary, get a dump truck and clean house.

Prayer

Father God, I repent and ask Your Son Jesus to come into my life right now. I choose to be born again as Nicodemus was. Indwell me and fill my life with Your sweet presence forever.

Thank You for speaking to me through the faithful Church of Smyrna. Help me be faithful to You, as they were.

Praise be to Almighty God: my Triune Lord.

Amen.

CHAPTER SIXTEEN

God's Woodshed

The Church of Pergamos

Sometimes the "Church" is taken to God's woodshed. This occurs when pastors get in the news, or are the subjects of local gossip sessions, due to running off with a congregant's spouse, for dishonesty in finances, or child abuse, for example.

We Christian laity at times are taken to Father's woodshed too. I know what that feels like, especially during a period of unbelief and worldliness in my college days.

Yet He is patient with us, until for the good of His ultimate plan the Ruler of Heaven and Earth has to act. He waits for us to repent, make restitution, and return to Father's House.

Jesus' Last Recorded Words

The last words an individual speaks are unbelievably important. Some of Jesus' last words on earth were, *"Behold, I send the Promise of My Father upon you; but tarry in the city of Jerusalem until you are endued with power from on high"* (Luke 24:49).

Incredibly important words! They were for me, personally, when I received the power of the Holy Spirit and spiritual gifts at age 26. (See Acts 2:1-4.)

Shortly after our Savior's ascension, we hear a reversed message, this time sent from Heaven to Earth. In a kind of Near-Death experience, the Apostle John is sent to Heaven long enough to hear Jesus give a last recordable message for earth.

You now have the opportunity to study these seven messages Jesus sent us through His Apostle John who wrote the Book of Revelation.

Thus far we have heard the messages to Ephesus, and Smyrna. What then does Jesus say to Pergamos (or Pergamum) a town in Mysia?

Affirmation

And to the angel of the church in Pergamos write: These things says He who has the sharp two-edged sword: I know your [good] works, and where you live, where Satan's throne is. And you hold fast to My name. You did not deny My faith even in the days in which Antipas was My faithful martyr, who was killed among you, where Satan dwells. (Revelation 2:12, 13)

• Works
• Holding fast to Christ's name
• Not denying the faith

The church in Pergamos was living in a very demonic location and yet doing good works for God's Kingdom. This was commendable. Where is Satan's seat? In 1878, the German engineer, Carl Human, discovered in Pergamum the huge altar of the Greek idol Zeus.[16] This idol was believed to be what Scripture referred to as "Satan's seat." It is now housed in Berlin; major archaeological campaigns have been conducted there.[17]

The Believers held fast to Christ's name and their faith even when there was the public burning of the Christian martyr Antipas. *Unger's Bible Dictionary* says of Antipas, "He is said to be one of our Savior's first disciples and a bishop of Pergamos … He lived before 100 A.D."

The book, *The Acts of Antipas* says about his death, "He was put to death by being enclosed in a burning brazen bull" (Dake, 1963, p. 287). What a place Antipas has in the history of the Church and in Heaven! Most people do not know his name now, but he will be known.

Yet this church of Pergamos is described, by commentators, as "The Compromising Church" because they tolerated immorality, idolatry, and heresies. This city was the combination of a pagan cathedral city, a university town, and a royal residence.

In business or family matters, there are times when you have to take a centrist or compromising position, but where your faith is concerned there must be no compromise.

Warning

Jesus said:

"But I have a few things against you because you have there those who hold the doctrine of Balaam, who taught Balak to put a stumbling block before the children of Israel, to eat things sacrificed to idols, and to commit sexual immorality." (Revelation 2:14)

The Message Bible puts it this way, *"But why do you indulge that Balaam crowd? Don't you remember that Balaam was an enemy agent, seducing Balak and sabotaging Israel's holy pilgrimage by throwing unholy parties? (Revelation 2:14).*

Balaam is a heathen prophet from the Midianites who has learned some of the ways of the Lord. His prophecies are sometimes valid and other times a mixture. He becomes well known, conceited, and covetous.

The story begins when the children of Israel, after a great victory against the Amorites, move into the plains of Moab (B.C.1401). Balak the King of Moab becomes afraid and sends a message to Balaam that he wants to hire him to curse the people of Israel so that Balak can defeat them.

Balaam prays to God regarding this tempting invitation three times, and each time God tells him he cannot curse those God has blessed. Finally, with permission by the Angel of the Lord, Balaam goes to the King of Moab and with animal offerings, four times, asks God for a word but each time it is a prophecy of blessing for Israel. The four prophecies are total blessings, and even seem to be prophetic for Israel today. The King is furious.

Balaam's Sin

Then Balaam chooses to accept the monetary bribe and recommends to the King of Moab a plan for Israel's defeat. It is the seduction of the men of Israel through marrying the idolatrous Moabite women. This sin of spiritual adultery brings Israel into defeat. (See Numbers 31:15, 16.)

How many men in our modern times have had similar temptation set-ups, by the Enemy, to bring about their spiritual defeat? Commercializing God's gifts for profit is another Balaam sin not to be deceived by today. I think this message of Balaam should be taught more in the 21st Century. (See Numbers, chapters 22 – 25.)

After many trials, Israel finally repents and is not totally defeated. Balaam is killed in war.

"The 'way of Balaam' (2 Peter 2:15) is the covetous conduct of the typical hireling prophet, solicitous only to commercialize his gift (Jude 11). ... Balaam as a prophet offers the strange spectacle of a prophet-diviner—a mixture of paganistic ritual with a true, though blurred, knowledge of the true God" (Ibid. Unger, p. 139).

Here again are those two sins that were prominent in Ephesus! They are evil deeds that separate God's human creation from their Creator.

The Pergamos culture was taught Balaam's teachings and Balak's example from hundreds of years before, to break God's Commandments, specifically numbers one, two, and seven:

"You shall not have another god before Me." "You shall not make unto yourselves any engraved image ... You shall not bow down to them nor serve them." "You shall not commit adultery (includes fornication)" (Exodus 20:4, 5, 14).

Nicolaitan Teaching Condemned

In addition Jesus says, once again, that He hates the doctrine of the Nicolaitans. We see the doctrine of this group condemned along with Balaam. They [the Nicolaitans] apparently believed that sexual immorality and ungodly behavior would not affect one's standing in Christ (i.e. his or her salvation). We know this to be a false doctrine because God says we are to *"follow after holiness, without which no man shall see the Lord"* (Hebrew 12:14). [18]

Repent

What is the remedy for all this? *"Repent, or else I will come to you quickly and will fight against them with the sword of My mouth"* (Revelation 2:16).

This church of Pergamos is in danger because some of them "hold the doctrine of the Nicolaitans" and they are teaching false doctrine leading God's people astray.

God the Son's mouth is like a two edged sword if we won't repent. The Scripture states, *"For the Word of God is living and powerful, and sharper than any two-edged sword ...* (Hebrews 4:12). Jesus came the first time gentle as a Lamb. Next time He will come as the Lion of Judah and our powerful King.

Repent if you are walking the same path as the Enemy of your soul. Repent means turn around and change directions. God wants to show you what real joy is. He wants to take away your loneliness, your addictions that are killing you, your lack of purpose in life. God's gift of forgiveness is such a wonderful gift and you can receive it anytime you are willing to follow Him.

Rewards

He who has an ear, let him hear what the Spirit says to the churches. To him who overcomes I will give some of the hidden manna to eat. And I will give him a white stone, and on the stone a new name written which no one knows except him who receives it. (Revelation 2:17)

- Hidden Manna to eat
- A white stone
- A new name—written on the stone

The author of Hebrews (9:4) includes a "golden jar holding manna" among the contents of the Ark of the Covenant for a memorial. It was a constant tradition of the Jews that the Ark, the tables of stone, Aaron's rod, the holy anointing oil, and the jar of manna were hidden by Josiah when Jerusalem was taken by the Chaldeans, and that these shall be restored in the days of the Messiah (Ibid. Unger, p. 813).

Revelation shows us that the Ark is in Heaven. "*Then the Temple of God was opened in Heaven, and the Ark of His covenant was seen in His Temple*" (Revelation 11:19). Wouldn't it be grand for the hidden manna to be used at a heavenly Communion service? This is a conjecture, but I believe that it will be "the food for those who are saved in the heavenly Kingdom" (Revelation 3:17, *The Jerusalem Bible*, p. 322, 323d).

On the occasion of receiving my master's degree in counseling in June 2008, the key note speaker, Nutritionist Graham Kerr, gave each graduate a flat, slate stone he called a skipping stone. It's fun to take a stone like that and skip it as far as you can over a body of water. Our lives are like skipping stones going out as far as we can, to grow and be successful in making this world a better place. Whenever I pick up this stone, I think of what it and that day means to me.

At a special time in Heaven, Jesus will give us a white stone, a token of acceptance that has our endearing new name inscribed on it. These were known to the ancients as victory stones. Also in ancient times, they meant pardon and the evidence of it. Judges had white and black stones. If a black one was given, the criminal was condemned; if a white one, he would be pardoned.

Conquerors in the public games were also given white stones with their names on them, which entitled them to be supported the rest of their lives at public expense (Dake, 1963, p. 287).

As the family of God, we will be taken care of not only in this life, but also for eternity. The white stone, meaning purity, is significant to overcomers and it is a love gift you and I will treasure, always.

A Moment to Reflect and Pray

Take a moment to think of what God has said to you. If you feel convicted, you only need to pray:

Dear Father God and Lord Jesus, please help me. Forgive me. I desperately need You. I humbly repent from my own sins and for leading others astray from You and into Balaam and Nicolaitan types of idolatry and sexual sins. Forgive me if I've engaged in the idolatry of pornography.

Cleanse me from the darkness that has crept into my soul and body. Thank You for showing me the way before it is too late. Help me to make restitution to anyone I've wounded.

Forgive me from abusing the gift of Grace and using it as a license to sin. I humbly repent. Show me what you want me to do to serve you the rest of my life. I choose to make You Lord of my life, Jesus. I forsake any false gods I've been involved with knowingly or unknowingly. Jesus is Lord! In Your Name, I pray. Amen.

Now wait in His presence and listen. When you can write down what you've heard. If you need extra help, get into a Believer's Support group and sign up for a Spirit-filled Bible Study. Also, seek the power of the Holy Spirit to strengthen you in your resolve to follow the Lord Jesus Christ.

CHAPTER SEVENTEEN

Good Works but Needs Word

The Church of Thyatira

We now begin an account of the fourth church that Christ speaks to as recorded in the Book of Revelation. It is in Thyatira, an ancient city in Asia Minor (located today in West Turkey). It was known as a church of extremely good works, always excelling in them.

Revelation of Jesus, Son of God
  • Eyes like a flame of fist—Eternal wisdom, judgment of evil
  • Feet like fine brass—unchanging
  And to the angel of the church in Thyatira write, "These things says the Son of God, who has eyes like a flame of fire, and His feet like fine brass: I know your works, love, service, faith, and your patience, and as for your works, the last are more than the first." (Revelation 2:18-19)

Affirmations of Overcomers
  • works
  • love
  • service
  • faith

- patience
- increased works

The church at Thyatira was commended for their works and charity. Unlike the church in Ephesus who had left their first love, this church was doing more now than at the beginning of their walk. But as we will soon see, increase of sacrifice is no substitute for obedience to the true Word of the Lord (www. truthablaze.com).

This church though doing noteworthy good works did not have the balance of being students of God's Word. As a result, it was eventually so influenced by the world in the marketplace that it eventually earned the infamous title of "The Corrupt Church."

Repent

After commending him (and the church) Jesus speaks strongly to the pastor of the Church in Thyatira, "But I have this against you, that you tolerate the woman Jezebel, who calls herself a prophetess, and she teaches and leads My bond servants astray, so that they commit acts of immorality and eat things sacrificed to idols." (Revelation 2:20 NASB)

This is not the wicked Jezebel, wife of King Ahab of Israel, but Jesus here is giving this title to the Thyatiran woman who exhibited similar unbiblical character traits.

This Jezebel from Asia Minor taught idolatry and adultery spiritually and physically, which means breaking the second and seventh Commandments of God as given to Moses on Mount Sinai (Exodus 20:1-17).

Bible scholar, Adam Clarke, believes that she was the wife of the messenger or bishop of the church of Thyatira. That is how she gained such influence. As the bishop he could have restrained her but he did not (Clark, p. 981).

The Temptation

What was the actual problem leading to this promiscuous living? History reveals that Christian workers had to join trade unions led by pagans. They would often meet at a pagan temple and begin with a libation to the gods. Licentious orgies were often connected to worship of erotic Greek idols.

The central problem for Thyatiran Christians was that they had to belong to a union in order to make a living. It seems Jezebel encouraged the workers to compromise, and taught that it was necessary for business and perhaps for church finances too.

Warning

Jesus says, *"And I gave her space to repent of her fornication: and she repented not"* (Revelation 2:21 KJV).

Clarke says of "fornication" that this word is used at times to indicate idolatrous spiritual fornication. In this context the sin is primarily against God. Eventually this sin could lead to sexual sins of fornication also, that is, sex outside of marriage.

Only God knows how long the space of repentance is for each believer. Peter says, *"The Lord is not slack concerning His promise, as some count slackness, but is longsuffering toward us, not willing that any should perish but that we should all come to repentance"* (2 Peter 3:9).

But the difference with Jezebel is she would not repent and apparently had no plans to. She had certainly moved far away from living as a Christian into the eventual danger of apostasy.

These kinds of activities are not only true of "Jezebels" today but one might call similar men "Johnibels." Pastors and counselors must be psychologically well, moral, and delivered from occult beliefs, before they are given responsibility of caring for the souls of needy, vulnerable individuals.

Warning Continues

Behold, I will cast her [Jezebel] upon a bed of sickness, and those who commit adultery with her into great tribulation, unless they repent of their deeds. And I will kill her [adult sons: Ahaziah; Johoram] children with pestilence; and all the churches will know that I am He who searches the minds and hearts; and I will give to each one of you according to your deeds." (Revelation 2:22,23 NASB)

Clarke believes the Scripture juxtapositions the two biblical stories of Jezebel No. 1 married to King Ahab (871 B.C., 1 Kings 16:31-32, 18:19) and Jezebel No. 2 married to the leader or Bishop of Thyatira (Revelation 2:20).

The previous Scripture of Revelation 2:22, 23 is greatly clarified by understanding the complete history. The young adult brothers Ahaziah and Johoram followed in their mother's occult practices and died unrepentant, as did their mother (Clarke, Vol. I, p. 981).

Some commentators do not believe there was a second Jezebel but that all the time this Scripture was referring to the original infamous person. I was relieved to read Clarke's commentary for the best historical clarity with two different women.

Jesus warns us, *"The thief does not come except to steal, and to kill, and to destroy, but I have come that they may have life, and that they may have it more abundantly"* (John 10:10).

I believe it was the Enemy who came to "steal, kill, and destroy" Ahaziah and Johoram. God had given them time to repent but because they were in occult behavior and surrounded by hundreds of prophets of Baal and prophets of Astarte, with no faith based foundation they were lost. They were **not** lost as **little children**, as some Bible translations misconstrue, but they died as responsible **young men**.

List of Contrasts of Two Jezebels
Jezebel No.1's sins:
1) Taking another god—broke 1st Commandment,
2) Fornication of Idolatry—broke 2nd Commandment,
3) Established Phoenician occult worship in King Ahab's court,
4) Taught her sons idolatry,
5) Promoted Gnostic beliefs,
6) When her teaching was opposed by the prophet of God, Elijah, she vowed to take his life (did not succeed),
7) Not willing to repent,
8) Possibly taught adultery,
9) Jezebel wrote a warrant, *in Ahab's name usurping his authority,* for the death of Naboth taking over his property; consequently she and Ahab fell under the prophet's curse. Jezebel had a very bad ending. (She had a weak husband.)

Jezebel No.2's sins:
1) Taking another god —broke 1st Commandment,
2) Fornication of Idolatry—broke 2nd Commandment,
3) Taught eating of food offered to idols—opening participants up to fellowshipping with demons,
4) Possibly taught adultery,
5) Taught *Gnosticism*
6) Not willing to repent. (She, too, had a weak husband.)

The Ten Commandments
First Century believers were taught the Ten Commandments in the Books of Moses (*Torah*). The Second Commandment warns against Idolatry: "You shall not make for yourself an idol in the form of anything in Heaven above or on the earth beneath or in the waters below. You shall not bow down to them or worship them; for I, the Lord your God, am a jealous God ..." (Exodus 20:4, 5, Kohlenberger III, *Hebrew-English Old Testament*, p. 200).

Why does God say He's jealous? Because His chosen people got into idolatry big time while Moses was seeking God on Mount Sinai.

The sin of idolatry or creating another god, a false god, is best represented in "the orgy of the Golden Calf." God had just brought the Children of Israel out of slavery in Egypt, and now they are committing spiritual adultery against God! (Exodus 32:1-25).

Dr. Laura says, "The Israelites after waiting forty days for Moses to come down from Mount Sinai, thought he was dead or had deserted them. They fell back into old patterns by building themselves a god representation—a golden calf. Idolatry, with its physical representation of gods, was so enticing to the Israelites that the prophets had to chastise the people about it repeatedly" (Schlessinger, 1998, p. 31).

What are idols particular to our day? One idol is pornography, especially of the female body, often smuggled into our homes by Internet. This is a big temptation for emotionally needy men or women. It can become an addiction, wastes a lot of time and money, sets a bad example for the children, eventually harm one's marriage, makes one vulnerable to spiritual attacks, and causes separation from God's presence. There are other effects you can think of.

Rewards

Jesus continues:

"But to you I say to the rest in Thyatira, as many as have not this teaching, who knew not the deep things of Satan, as they say: I am not casting on you another burden; nevertheless what you have hold until I shall come." (Revelation 2:24, 25, Marshall, p. 963)

- Not giving you a burden
- What you have, hold until I come

Commentators believe Jesus is speaking of the teaching of *Gnosticism* by Jezebel. *"Gnosticism*, a name indicating the assumption of superior knowledge (Gr. *gnosis*, knowledge). *Gnosticism* in its diverse forms received its impulse, and in the main its guidance, from pagan philosophy. In different ways it denied the humanity of Christ, even to the extent of denying the reality of His human body" (Ibid. Unger, p. 614).

Commentator Adam Clarke says the Gnostic's intent is by their secret craft to undermine the Christian religion. He says further, "It is worthy of remark that the Gnostics called their doctrine *the depths of God, and the depths of Bythos,* intimating that they contained the most *profound secrets of Divine wisdom.* Christ here calls them the *depths of Satan,* being masters of subtlety" (Clark, *Commentary*, p. 982).

Christ's words for the overcoming believers are: "I am not casting on you another burden; nevertheless what you have hold until I shall come" (Marshall, *Greek-English*, 1964, p. 963).

In other words, God the Son has shared quite a bit of heavy information with you! That's all you need for now as you have a lot to absorb. Keep faithful and hold on to what you have until He comes.

Have you noticed that God's Words often show themselves as outside of time, even as eternity is timeless? Your spirit where God's Spirit dwells is the part of you that can best have "ears to hear" what God's Spirit says to the Church.

"He who is joined to the Lord is one Spirit with Him" (1Corinthians 6:17). You are spirit, soul, and body. Your born again spirit, confirmed by the sixty-six books of the Bible, will lead you in God's truth.

Your spirit (*ruach* or *pneuma*), joined to the Spirit of the Lord desires to inform your soul (*nephesh* or *psyche*). Your soul (mixture of good and evil) that is in the process of sanctification desires to inform your body (bodily, sensual nature). We must live from the Spirit in order to hear from the Lord most clearly.

A Scotsman was riding his donkey and having a nice day. As he rode over a small bridge the donkey's hoof got caught in the foothold. The man yelled at the donkey, "*Laddie*, if you're going to get on, I'm going to get off!" We need to guard against human beings carnal, animal nature getting into the saddle.

The Blessed Remnant

I do not know how the Thyatiran Believers survived in this culture, but the good news is that *a remnant* of them remained faithful.

The Apostle Paul visited Thyatira at least three times on his missionary journeys and some of this "remnant" were likely his converts. In the church at Philippi of Macedonia there was a woman named Lydia, a seller of purple clothing who had moved there from Thyatira. Through the ministry of Paul, her heart was opened to the Lord and her whole family came into the faith. (See Acts 16:14-15.) It is good to have a contrast between the obedient Lydia, and the disobedient, idolatrous "twin" Jezebels.

Rewards Continued

Jesus' second list of promises to the overcomer are:

"And the one overcoming and the one keeping until the end the works of Mine, I will give him authority over the nations, and he will shepherd them with an iron staff, as the vessels—clay are broken, as I also have received from the Father of Mine, and I will give him the Morning Star." (Revelation 3:26-28, mod: Marshall, *Interlinear Greek*, 1964, p. 963)

- Authority over the nations—in the millennium
- The Morning Star—Christ the greatest reward

Here we see Jesus speaking prophetically about the righteous Thyatirans one day "ruling and reigning" with Christ in the millennial Kingdom. I like the *Interlinear Greek* gentleness of Jesus' Words speaking of the clay vessels that are broken. It's like He's speaking about working with rebelliously difficult people being broken so He, the Great Potter, can lovingly yet surgically mold those broken pieces into works of art and service. He doesn't crush, but if allowed, He will make something beautiful out of any broken clay who will allow it.

He is the "Morning Star." He will give you Himself, His abiding and awesome presence for eternity. He brings daylight, and sunshine into your spirit, soul, and body that will shine out to the world. He is your ultimate reward.

This Epistle ends with the usual demand for attention to Christ's Words. *"He that has an ear, let him hear what the Spirit says to the churches"* (Revelation 2:29).

A Moment to Reflect and Pray

Has the Lord spoken to you through this Epistle? Take a moment to write down what you've learned that has impressed you. Are you one of the faithful? Is there anything God has shown you to confess to Him with a repentant heart?

As believers, we need to check our hearts and souls daily to see if we are up to speed with God's living Word. Specifically check on this with His Ten Commandments, for example (Exodus 20: 1-17). Are there any Jezebels or Johnibels you need to pray for that you're concerned about?

Pray for your church home that it will be fed spiritually and told the truth from the God's Word. What can you do to help them? Pastors and Rabbis need all the help they can get, to assist the flock. Some people need healing physically or emotionally. Keeping confidentiality; you can fast a few meals and get alone with God to prayerfully make special intentions for those you see have a need.

Dear Father God,

Search my heart so that I may see if there is any sin there that I have not offered to You. Reveal my needs to me. I want to please You and follow in Your footsteps. Show me the next footprints I should make on Planet Earth.

I want Your Kingdom to expand, and the Enemy's failed kingdom to recede. It is happening but it seems not enough when I read the paper or see the news.

Help me as I pray, sing, and meditate on *The Lord's Prayer* daily to help bring Your Kingdom to earth. *"Thy Kingdom come on Earth as it is in Heaven"* (Matthew 6:9-13).

May I be ready for whatever you call me to do. Assist me in becoming a strong student of the Bible—Genesis to Revelation. May I find my calling in your true Church, the body of Messiah, that the Gates of Hell cannot prevail against (Matthew 16:18). In Jesus Christ's Name.

Amen.

CHAPTER EIGHTEEN

Holy Spirit Revives

The Church of Sardis

What can make a person who was once alive in his faith change so drastically that he is inwardly dead? To have once known the source of life, God himself, and then be convinced that there is no God is to turn out the light that once glowed in one's spirit.

This does not happen in a moment of time. Unbelief is a slow, steady process. Just as an individual has to feed his body to live, so it is necessary for him to feed his soul—intellect, emotions and will—good food, both spiritually and psychologically.

If, like the *Sardinians*, you are beginning to cool off in your relationship to your Creator, now would be a good time to change your spiritual diet. Let me tell you what happened to them.

The City of Sardis

The chief city of Lydia, Sardis, was located at the junction of royal highways linking Ephesus, Pergamum, and Smyrna with the interior of Asia Minor. Sardis was situated in a valley among almost impregnable cliffs.

Sardis was famous for its arts and crafts, as well as its dyeing and woolen industries. Because of its natural resources, it was the first center to mint gold and silver coins. The earliest reference to Sardis is in the *Persae* of Aeschylus, 472 B.C.

This epistle to Sardis, as with all seven letters, was written prophetically through the Apostle John on the Isle of Patmos 96 A.D. (Dake p. 305). It was then delivered, as best we can surmise, around that time or as soon as he could send it by boat across the Aegean Sea. It was delivered by the Roman mailman on horseback. Not an easy feat. And here you are 2,000 years later reading the letters too!

In Jesus Christ's epistle to Sardis, as usual, He addresses it to the pastor (angel) of the Church living in that city. *"And to the angel of the church in Sardis write, These things says He who has the seven Spirits of God and the seven stars, 'I know your works, that you have a name that you are alive, but you are dead'"* (Revelation 3:1). What a shocking statement from the One who knows all hearts.

Jesus Begins with a Warning
- Works are negative.
- False reputation of life.
- Truth "You're dead."

"Sardis is said to be the first city in that part of the world that was converted by the preaching of John; and, some say, the first that revolted from Christianity. The Lord Jesus, by whom this message was sent—"that has the seven spirits of God, and the seven stars."

(1) "He has the seven spirits, that is, the Holy Spirit with His various powers. This epistle being sent to a languishing ministry and church, they are very fitly put in mind that Christ has the seven spirits, [that is] the Spirit without measure and in perfection, to whom they may apply themselves for the reviving of the work among them.

(2) "He has the seven stars, the angels of the churches. The Holy Spirit usually works by the ministry, and the ministry will

be of no efficacy without the Spirit; the same divine hand holds them both" (Henry, 1961, p. 1972-1973, mod.).

In Review

Ephesus needed renewed love of their Savior Jesus and to do first works,

Pergamos needed to put away the occult and spiritual compromise,

Thyatira needed to put away spiritual fornication of idolatry and receive the life changing study of God's Word, and

Sardis needed reviving from Near-Death and infusion of the seven-fold empowerment of the Holy Spirit.

All these churches needed to repent. Repent isn't just saying lightly, "I'm sorry." But it is forsaking the sinful behavior that is plaguing you and keeping you earthbound.

Smyrna, thus far, is the only church that is not corrected by Jesus.

The Temptations for Sardis

"Sardis was known for its infamous Temple of Cybele, a fertility goddess known as the Great Mother. [Why does that sound familiar to me in our day?] The Temple of Cybele and the Temple of Artemis were located in the same area of the city. Sex orgies that sometimes included castration and mutilation were practiced among those who worshiped Cybele" (Barnhart, 2007, p. 389).

Here we again have breaking the Commandments: Having other gods before God, worshiping idols, and having sex orgies of fornication and adultery in this demonic atmosphere. Commandments 1, 2, and 7 are all broken here at the same time.

We do not know how many from the Christian community slipped over into this wild living, but obviously it had a deadening effect. The Apostle Paul warned believers, *"What? Know you not that your body is the temple of the Holy Spirit who is in you, that you have of God, and you are not your own? For you are bought with a price ...*" (I Corinthians 6:19, 20a KJV, mod.).

Needing Holy Spirit Power

The Sardinians needed the power of the Spirit to deliver and revive them. The Hebrew name for the Holy Spirit is literally *Ruach hakodesh*, "Spirit the Holy." *Ruach* means breath. If you are a corpse, you need *ruach*, breath, or spirit.

At Pentecost, exactly fifty days after Jesus' resurrection, the power of the Holy Spirit came upon the 120 believers waiting in the Upper Room. They received the Baptism with the Holy Spirit and began to speak in languages they had never learned as they extolled God beyond their limited human understanding (Acts 2:1-4).

This is when the Church blasted off from the mundane to the colossal. No one in that Upper Room in Jerusalem could remain half-dead or asleep after that. They burst out of the upstairs, ran down and out to the sidewalks so filled with the love of God that some observers thought they were drunk even though it was only *Nine O'clock in the Morning*. Being filled with the New Wine of the Holy Spirit is the best of all parties!

This is what the Church of Sardis needed. The *Acts of the Apostles* written through "the beloved physician" Luke about 62 A.D. might not have made it to Asia in written scroll form by then. But the Apostle Paul had been with the seven churches several times and most likely the Good News would have spread.

Repent

Jesus gives commands to Sardis:

"*Be watchful, and strengthen the things which remain, that are ready to die, for I have not found your works perfect before God. Remember how you have received and heard; hold fast and repent.*" (Revelation 3:2,3a)

The Spirit is obviously needed when Jesus says, "*Strengthen the things which remain and are ready to die* [to expire]." We need the empowering strength of the Spirit and the breath of life so we will not die spiritually. We must keep inspired.

Also Jesus says, "*Remember how you have received and heard.*"

It is important for us to continue to be willing to tell our story of our Holy Romance with God's Son. How and where were you when you received Eternal Life and the power of the Holy Spirit? Who helped you? It is so inspiring to tell others about what God has done for you and review it again to yourself. Witnessing and praying for others are two of my favorite activities. I do not believe a church will continue to be dead when the congregation is so inspired with the Holy Spirit.

One of my recent witnessing encounters was while I was at Starbucks enjoying a latte. I was reading *The Edmonds Beacon* to see how my latest column came out. I kept hearing two men, a senior and a junior, having a heated discussion. I kept hearing the words "Jesus" and "Jesus Christ." I could not tell in what context these words were being used.

I closed my eyes to pray and got the idea to go by their table and offer them my paper to read as I had been doing a series on *The Beatitudes*. Gathering up my courage I walked up to their table and I said, "Hi, I kept hearing the name of my best friend, Jesus, being mentioned over here and thought I'd drop by to say, 'Hello.'"

The young man invited me to sit down with them as he was explaining the Bible to his elder friend. It was a most interesting discussion and forty-five minutes later I had a chance to pray with the older gentleman to make sure he had opened the door of his heart to his Savior Jesus. He was visibly moved and so was I.

Surprisingly the young man looked up at me and said, "I needed you." I smiled and said, "Thank you very much." I said my goodbyes to my new brothers then I shopped for my needed groceries in record speed. As I drove home, I was singing and rejoicing. Spirit-led times like this are so inspiring to me!

Warning: Watch and Pray

Jesus continues to warn, *"Therefore if you will not watch, I will come upon you as a thief, and you will not know what hour I will come upon you"* (Revelation 3:3b). Finis Dake says, "This does not refer to the Second Advent, but to Christ sending sudden judgment upon Sardis" if they will not repent" (Dake, 1963, p. 288).

Jesus' warning to the church that if they will not repent He will come upon them as a thief in the night, reminds me of a possible prophetic word for us two millennia later with His sudden appearing in the clouds at the end of the age. In the Gospel of Matthew, Jesus says

"Watch therefore, for you do not know what hour your Lord is coming. But know this, that if the master of the house had known what hour the thief would come, he would have watched and not allowed his house to be broken into." (Matthew 24:42,43; see also 1 Thessalonians 5:1-13)

Rewards for Overcomers

Our Lord goes on to commend the Remnant, *"You have a few names even in Sardis who have not defiled their garments; and they shall walk with Me in white, for they are worthy"* (Revelation 3:4). These believers in "white linen garments" are those whose spotted garments have been washed white from sins, by the blood of the Lamb, Jesus. These believers have eternal life, and will walk with Christ in His Kingdom. Adam and Eve walked with God in the Garden in the cool of the day. You and I will walk with God too. This time it may be near the River of Life and our talk with Him may include picking and eating ripe fruit from the Tree of Life.

More Rewards

Jesus concludes with other rewards for Overcomers:

He who overcomes shall be clothed in white garments, and I will not blot out his name from the Book of Life; but I will confess his name before My Father and before His angels. (Revelation 3:5)

- Clothed in white garments
- Name in the Lamb's Book of Life
- Name confessed before Father God and His angels

He or she will be dressed in shining white garments, which represents the righteousness of the saints. The white garments also indicate those who while on earth helped the needy. *"Inasmuch as you did it to one of the least of these My brethren, you did it to Me,"* said Jesus (Matthew 25:40b).

Your name is written in the Lamb's Book of Life. There is no danger of having your name blotted out of the Book of Life once you have accepted Jesus Christ as your Savior, repented of your sins, and forsaken them.

The main danger of a name being blotted out of the Book of Life is apostasy; that is, one denying the Lord who saved him or her and continuing in that state until death. The example of Jezebel shows one who heard the truth, but we are told in Scripture, she would not repent. I leave the final judgment to God himself, who alone is the Judge of all.

And how awesome it is to have your name confessed before Father God by His Son. Imagine the Lord Jesus saying to His Father, this is Jane, or John, (fill in your name) one of your dear children from earth. Then having Father and Jesus giving you great big hugs rather than regular handshakes. How about when our Lord introduces you to the Archangels, Michael and Gabriel? How about Mary and Joseph? The Apostles? We have so many amazing adventures ahead of us, don't we?

God's Word Brings Life

A lifestyle of Bible study throughout your days on earth is vitally important. Don't waste your life reading murder mysteries, gambling at casinos, or watching TV. What will you have to talk about when you see Jesus? Imagine a conversation with Him on one of those topics.

We do not give God much of a chance to change us when we spend forty hours a week at work, twenty-five hours a week watching TV, reading the paper and other periodicals, listening to the radio and paying bills, answering emails, exercising, fifty hours a week sleeping, twenty-five hours with your family, eating, talking, playing, bathing, and two hours a week at church with fifteen minutes for Scripture reading, a twenty-minute sermon, and thirty minutes for Holy Communion, five minutes of prayer at the altar, and one hour at coffee time visiting with your friends.

As good as this is, it is not enough to get you ready to do your best to live your days for Christ in this life and get you ready for your eternal Home. Adding a powerful, Spirit-led, biblical seminar several times a year would help to give you more spiritual input and empowerment. The more spiritual food you receive, like this, the more you'll realize how to inject further spiritual life into your schedule. In fact, you'll hunger for it.

One weekend my late husband, Dennis, and I took my widowed father to a Christian Retreat Center in Bradenton, Florida, where both of us were teaching. Except for meals, all day my dad, William Harvey Reed, heard songs of praise and worship, and life giving messages inspired by the Word of God. His cup was full and running over with peace and joy.

When I saw him the next morning he said, "Rita, last night as I woke up off and on, I'd hear songs and praises coming back to me. When I awoke this morning I had the same experience." He had a big smile on his dear face. I was so happy for his response.

With all the bad news we absorb from the media, it's no wonder that many people are depressed. It is not that we should totally ignore the news, but we should balance it out with the Good News God has for us. Don't keep playing in the minor key on the piano all the time.

What Happened to Sardis?

Here's some history. A surprise attack by the Persians came in 549 B.C., and about three centuries later the Romans won Sardis in 133 B.C. The great earthquake of 17 A.D. ruined Sardis physically and financially for many years, though the Emperor Tiberius helped rebuild the city. They must have recovered to a large extent before the Apostle John wrote to them near the end of the first century.

Finally, Sardis was destroyed by Tamerlane, a Mongol conquer, in 1402 A.D. Apparently, today a modern town of Sart is located near where Sardis once was.[19]

When a nation walks with God, we know that is a good way to have His help. America started out this way, but how far have we strayed from the beliefs of our founding Fathers? How spotted are our garments? How happy is our Lord to see that lotteries and casinos are promoted as good ways to help our economy?

The Best Kind of Change

Change starts with one person at a time. It begins with me and it begins with you. Wouldn't it be a good idea for us today to make a resolution to follow Christ's commands for the church in Sardis, and all the other churches of Revelation?

Can we review our nation's history and see why we are great, and where we have begun to go astray?

Politically in 2008, most everyone was talking about change. But can't we also work for something even greater—spiritual change, eternal change? In doing so, you can have the best life now, and later.

Reach out your hand to touch the Hand that is reaching out to you. Our Lord will guide you all the way. He loves you and wants the best for you.

Revelation of Christ
- Son of Man walking in the churches
- Wearing a long white robe
- A gold band around His chest

God's Golden Menorah in Heaven
John the Apostle saw an amazing sight in Heaven:

I turned around to see who was speaking to me; and when I had turned, I saw seven gold menorahs; and among the menorahs someone like a Son of Man, wearing a robe down to his feet and a gold band around his chest. (Revelation 1:12,13, *Complete Jewish Bible*)

This Bible translation clarifies that there was not just one *menorah* with seven oil lamps to represent the seven churches, but each of the seven churches had an individual menorah with seven lamps. That makes forty-nine oil lamps ablaze and Jesus the light of earth and Heaven walking among the church *menorahs*! What a picture is this glorious plethora of menorahs with Christ in the midst.

Meditation on Isaiah 11:2
There are various menorah groups of sevens in the Bible. One I like especially is Isaiah 11:2, as it gives the characteristics of the Holy Spirit. Here the Prophet Isaiah shows the seven

menorah lamps as: wisdom and understanding, counsel and might, Spirit of knowledge of the Lord and fear of the Lord, and the Lord God himself in the center of the menorah. We will look at them from right to left as Hebrew is written and read; the center lamp is called *Shamish*.

We can see Jesus lighting the lamps in the Temple of our spirit. "You, Lord Jesus, are the center lamp, who desires to light up our lives, our Menorahs. With Your fire You light Wisdom to the far right, and Understanding to Your far left. How we need them both as they burn brightly reflecting one another. *"Get wisdom, get understanding: forget it not"* (Proverbs 4:5).

In the right middle, You light the special lamp of Counsel. We see it flare out in joy. May it burn brightly as we are dedicated to healing hearts and souls. May the Spirit of Counsel help spread Your light into the growing darkness of this fallen world!

Then we see You lighting the middle lamp on the left, that of Power. We must have Your Power to follow You and to help others on the pathway with us. Keep us filled with the power of the Holy Spirit so the *dunamous* burns brightly.

Now we are ready for You to light the gifts of Knowledge of the Lord on the right side center. We will be forever learning more and more about You. You are like a many faceted diamond with new viewpoints of knowledge of You that we can see and experience day by day.

And to the left center, Reverence and Awe for the Lord. Help me to not get overly familiar with You so that I take You for granted. As my Betrothed, I hold you in Reverence and Awe, while at the same time loving You as my Best Forever Friend.

A Moment to Reflect and Pray:

Take a few minutes to meditate and think about what God has said to you concerning this teaching of Sardis. Write it down when you can to help your further prayer time.

Check to see if there is any deadness in your soul. Pray as David did: *"Search me, O God, and know my heart: Try me, and know my anxieties; And see if there is any wicked way in me, And lead me in the way everlasting"* (Psalm 139:23,24).

Prayer

By faith, Dear Lord, I see all the lamps are lit in the Temple of my spirit. May they burn brightly to light my home, church, and work place. When I counsel, witness, teach, listen, pray with others, may my inner lamps burn more brightly to shed Your light into the life of friend or stranger.

You are awesome Lord! This room is full of Your holy light. Walk among us Christ, Messiah, as You walked among the menorahs of the seven Churches of Revelation. Search our hearts and souls to purify. May we learn the lessons the churches failed and rejoice in the lessons they learned.

May we have better discernment in our own church home, or Judeo-Christian community, for what we need to do to be more pleasing to You. Help our church or community be one You are proud of.

I know You will send help to answer this prayer, Lord Jesus.

Amen.

CHAPTER NINETEEN

City of Brotherly Love

The Church of Philadelphia

Of the seven churches mentioned in Revelation, only Philadelphia and Smyrna (previously discussed) received praise and no correction from Christ. We've studied the second church, Smyrna, the persecuted church, and now we will find out about the sixth church, Philadelphia, and see why it was so honored (Revelation 3:7-13).

The home of the church of Philadelphia was located in "a city in Lydia of Asia Minor. The Church of St. John dating to the eleventh century is there."

Philadelphia was built by Attalus II Philadelphus of the Kingdom of Pergamum, in B.C. 189. Because of the founder's love for his brother Eumenes II, the city is called Philadelphia—meaning "City of brotherly love" (Unger, 1988, p. 999, 1000).

The modern city of Philadelphia, known today as Alasehir, has a population of about 20,000 inhabitants.

Brotherly Love

When is the last time you went to church and experienced brotherly or sisterly love? The name of this fellowship "Church of Brotherly Love" reflects their consistent loving behavior and it was so called because it was established in a city by that very same name. Was that a coincidence or a God-incidence?

The Bible sometimes speaks of Jesus as our older Brother. One reference is Romans 8:29 that says, *"… God the Father, preordained His followers to be conformed to the image or likeness of His Son. And decreed that Jesus is the firstborn of many brothers and sisters."*

When He rose from the dead and breathed resurrection life into His apostles, they were the first group to experience spiritual resurrection. A new spiritual race of people began. The family has been growing ever since. What an fabulous big Brother we have in Jesus, who came all the way from one of the many star lit universes to rescue us. He is a friend who *"sticks even closer than a brother"* (Proverbs 18:24).

Revelation of Jesus Christ

We begin the letter from the Lord Jesus, spoken to John. In the words given to the pastor of the church of Philadelphia a powerful, fourfold description of the Christ is painted.

"And to the angel of the church in Philadelphia write,

These things says …

1. "He who is holy,
2. "He who is true,
3. "He who has the key [authority as did King David] of David,
4. "He who opens and no one shuts, and shuts and no one opens" (Revelation 3:7)

Though Jesus proclaims His earthly life as, *"I am the root and the offspring of David"* (Revelation 22:16); in His divinity following His resurrection, He proclaims himself beyond this as, *"All authority has been given to Me in Heaven and on earth"* (Matthew 28:18b).

Affirmations

To the Church of Philadelphia Jesus says, *"I know your works: see, I have set before you an open door … For you have*

a little strength, and have kept My Word, and have not denied My Name" (Revelation 3:8).
- Good works
- You have an open door
- You have a little strength
- You have kept My Word
- Have not denied My Name

Good works: The Philadelphian's were people of good works in the community and strong students of God's Word. In those early days, they studied mainly the Books of Moses, and probably portions of the Psalms and John and Paul's writings in scroll form.

Have an open door: This can be speaking of missionary endeavors. There are many examples of this in the Scriptures. At one point, St. Paul was, "forbidden by the Holy Spirit to preach in Asia," then they wanted to go to Bithynia: "but the Spirit suffered them not," while they were in Troas, "a vision appeared to Paul in the night": *"A man of Macedonia stood, and pleaded with him, saying, Come over into Macedonia, and help us"* (Acts 16:9).

Well, they went immediately to Macedonia and conversions, deliverances, and temporary imprisonment occurred. God opened and closed doors to Paul consistently. (Acts 16:6-9, see also verses10-40). Paul and his team had so many exciting experiences being led by the Holy Spirit that it is amazing.

Most of us Christians today have seen how God opens and closes doors for us. His guidance is amazing.

Have a little strength: Though weak numerically, they were strong in confessing and not denying the One whom they served.

Have kept My Word: They were faithful to God's Word. The books of the Bible then were mainly the Books of Moses, the Psalms, Proverbs, Isaiah, Gospel of John and perhaps other Gospel accounts, probably Matthew, some of Paul's

Epistles, Letters from John in Revelation. This is just a guess, but whatever scrolls they had or could look at in their church, they respected and revered as God's Words to them. Scripture was written by hand. Some could not read and so memorized what they heard.

Not denied Jesus' Name: Even the Apostle Peter denied that he knew Jesus, just hours before the crucifixion. Fortunately Peter had a chance to repent following Christ's resurrection (Timothy 2:12). Perhaps you and I haven't always stood up for Christ as we could have. How thankful we are for the grace of God and the gift of repentance.

A News Report: Modern Day Philadelphians

It's 7:00 in the evening. Down by the corner, there's a cluster of young boys hanging out. Everyone else stays inside—and for good reason. Suddenly... *Men United* roar up in a caravan of vans and jeeps, a rap song blasting from loudspeakers.

Like a group of gang enforcers, nine men in baseball caps and bomber jackets emerge and quickly spread to the various corners—approaching the boys. They are likely the only ones on the streets without guns. They pack pamphlets instead.

"How you all doing?" says Ray Jones, a sprightly leader of the group, approaching the cluster of boys who peer at him coldly.

"We're with *Men United for a Better Philadelphia,* a non-violence group. If you were expecting a drive-by, this is a love-by."

They have helped thousands. Violence has dropped. (Catherine Porter, *The Toronto Star,* January 10, 2006.)

"Men United" have probably never read about the ancient church of Philadelphia, yet they are practicing its teachings in

the City of Philadelphia, USA. Undoubtedly, their expressions of Brotherly Love have God's attention!

Let us also go and do the works of the Philadelphians, past and present.

Have a Servant's Heart

Indeed I will make those of the synagogue of Satan, who say they are Jews and are not, but lie–indeed I will make them come and bow down at your feet, and to know that I have loved you. (Revelation 3:9, NASB)[20]

Please read the reference to a similar concern written previously in Revelation 2:9 (church of Smyrna). There are those then, and now, who call themselves Christians who are not really believing Christians. And there are those who call themselves Jews who are not really believing Jews. In my example, both groups can be lying for their own advantage, or at best are simply ignorant of the terms they are using.

It hurts Jesus to see us treat one another disrespectfully. We are to only worship God not one another, but He wants us to stand before one another in brotherly love as the church of Philadelphia was exhibiting. Our Jewish Lord Jesus *(Yeshua)*, wants us to understand and love the race He chose to be born into and to know that He loves all of us the same. He came to save us all.

Before our Lord's crucifixion, He washed His disciples' feet and thereby encouraged them (and us) to have Servant Hearts.

Rewards

Then we have the question about what Jesus means when He says, *"Because you have kept My command to persevere, I also will keep you from the hour of trial which shall come upon the whole world, to test those who dwell on the earth"* (Revelation 3:10).

• You kept my command to persevere
• I will keep you from the hour of trial on the whole world

First of all, literally speaking, the early Church had terrible persecutions and they were just getting started in the first century. Eleven of Jesus Apostles were martyred and John the twelfth was exiled from his homeland of Israel and forced to live on the tiny Isle of Patmos as a prisoner.

The miracle is that John lived until a ripe old age. His main mission was being an apostle of Jesus, and then writing: The Gospel of John, 1st, 2nd, and 3rd Epistles of John, and the Book of Revelation.

This verse is considered by many biblical scholars to speak of trials that would come upon the seven representative churches, and perhaps others, in John's day.

Prophetic Words

Again, being two thousand years later, Jesus' Words could also be prophetic for the day in which we live. They could speak to us in particular about the "hour of the trial which shall come upon the whole world." This sounds like Luke 21:35 *"For as a snare shall it come on all them that dwell on the face of the whole earth."*

For those who have studied the Book of Daniel, it's hard not to think about a connection with the upcoming seventieth week of Daniel, or the "time of Jacob's trouble" when reading these words.

That last week of Daniel is called a Sabbatical Week, which is a week of seven years (9:27). Interestingly, the recent "Sabbatical Cycle" actually began October 1, 2008 on the Hebrew New Moon Calendar as seen from Jerusalem. This location, the most valid one, is where Jesus would have witnessed and celebrated *Yom Terurah—Feast of Trumpets* annually.

The proposed date on our Gregorian calendar was September 28, 2008, and September 29, 5768, on the Jewish calendar, but both missed it by a few days. The seven-year cycle ends at the new moon around September 15, 2015, and a new one begins.

No one can say that this upcoming seven year period is more significant than another, but the signs of the times seem more significant daily. I think more than ever it is important to be a student of the Bible and of one's Judeo biblical roots.

It also helps to understand how the Bible explains those mysterious three and one-half year dates in Revelation. The "fifth Gospel" or final book of the Bible is good to study for clues as to where we are in history today (Church, *Fall 2008 Sabbatical season of seven years began*, p. 3-4, p. 34-36).

I am not a pre-trib or mid-trib believer. But since I've learned from Rev. J. R. Church about the Sabbatical years, at the beginning of *Yom Terurah* (*Rosh HaShanna*) I take time to prayerfully seek the Lord. If He doesn't come then (He didn't this year—Fall 2008), I consider three and one-half years forward into mid-trib.

If then another cycle begins, the watchful believer can joyfully continue to expect Jesus to return. The Bible says this keeps us from temptation. I quote the Apostle John here:

"Beloved, now are we the sons of God, and it does not yet appear what we shall be: but we know that, when He shall appear, we shall be like Him; for we shall see Him as He is. And every man that has this hope in Him purifies himself, even as He is pure." (1 John 3:2, 3, (KJV, mod.)

We in the USA have certainly had more than our share of severe trials in recent years: The 9/11 disaster—four terrorist stolen "suicide" airliners were crashed in New York City,

Washington D.C., and Pennsylvania—killed 2,974 people and cost billions of dollars of office space and economy in lower Manhattan, which is only a small amount of the estimated expense (2001) (*Wikipedia*). Asian tsunami: 225,000 dead, U.S. assisted recovery (2004). Effects of Katrina Cyclone: 1,836 dead, 1,300 children missing, 6,600 people still missing, cost $81.2 billion U.S. dollars, one of five deadliest tropical cyclones in U.S. history (2005) *(Ibid)*. Global warming is a great concern (CNN 2006). Gas and oil prices (2007, 2008), housing mortgages, bank failures (2008), and the Wall Street Financial freefall (FOX News 2008).

Warning

Jesus continues speaking, *"Behold, I am coming quickly! Hold fast to what you have, that no one may take your crown [reward]"* (Revelation 3:11).

Commentator Finis Dake says this is: "A reference to the rapture [from: *raptura* Latin, *nazal* Heb.], for this is the coming of Christ the Church will experience before the Second Advent" (p. 288).

Christ will come "quickly" for His body of believers. That is not everyone will see it. Elsewhere He describes this event "as a thief" in quickness.

> *The dead in Christ shall rise first, then we who are alive and remain shall be caught up in the clouds, to meet the Lord in the air: and so shall we ever be with the Lord. Wherefore comfort one another with these words.* (I Thessalonians 4:16a-18 KJV)

At the Second Coming or Second Advent, it's different than the "catching away" as everyone will see it. *"Behold, He is coming with clouds, and every eye will see Him, even they who pierced Him. And all the tribes of the earth will mourn because of Him. Even so, Amen"* (Revelation 1:7).

In essence, the entire human race had part in the crucifixion of Jesus, so we all need to repent. Fortunately, for those who have repented from original sin, and accepted God's Son who died for us, we are totally forgiven, forever. Our daily sins are forgiven as we turn from them in repentance (1 John 1:9). Anyone can do this in his or her own words.

Let No One Take Your Crown:
How could anyone take your crown? Who are they? Those not interested in the Kingdom of God and not wanting you to be either. They want company in their utterly earthly and worldly pursuits. Crown stealers are people who tempt you with age-old lines: "But everyone is doing it. Just one time won't hurt." Or "Marriage is old-fashioned; you should have gotten over that idea years ago." Or "Everyone is a little dishonest; you can cheat on this contract and no one will know it. Let me show you how" (Bennett, 1997, p. 142).

There are five crowns listed in Scripture: Watcher's Crown, Soul Winner's Crown, Crown of Purity, Shepherd's Crown, and Crown of Life (Bennett, R., Crowns, p. 133-142).

Christians look at the "rapture" in different ways. Fortunately, there is no prerequisite on this subject for salvation, and no believer should predict a time. Nevertheless, we need to be students of the Bible so we'll at least have an inkling of what is going on when we compare the Morning News with the "Good News."

When Jesus teaches the parable of the wise and foolish virgins only five out of ten were watching and ready. He ends with, "Watch therefore, for you know neither the day nor the hour in which the Son of Man is coming" (Matthew 25:13).

Messiah Comes
Every year in Jerusalem, on *Yom Terruah*, "The Feast of Trumpets" (and *Rosh Hashanah*, their second New Year), it is reported that some Orthodox Jews go through the Market Place

shouting, *"Mashiach Bah Ah."* That is translated "Messiah is Coming." I was blown away when I heard this. These Orthodox Jews are more excited about Messiah's coming than some Christians are! The Jews study the *Seven Feasts of God*, which spans the Bible from Genesis to Malachi. We Christians can take the study all the way to Revelation, in fact, the last three feasts—yet to be fulfilled—are found there.

The Seven Feasts or Festivals of God, listed in Leviticus 23, give us a preview of the entire Bible. They begin at Passover *Pasach* (Salvation) and go to Tabernacles *Sukkot* (Messiah Jesus reigns on earth).

"All God's plan from chaos to eternity is ingeniously revealed through the nature of timing of these seven annual feasts" (Levitt, 1979, p.1). It is important for us to know that we are presently living between the fourth and fifth feasts: Pentecost and Trumpets.

Spirit-filled biblical Christians look for Christ (Messiah in Greek) to come a second time. Orthodox Jews are looking for the Messiah (*Ha Mashiach,* in Hebrew) to come the very first time.

Whether our Lord comes for us, or we go to Him, it would do us well to follow the example of this early Church or Synagogue (*Beit Kennesset*, Heb.) of Brotherly Love.

By the way, have you hugged your brother or your sister lately? Let's you and I talk to our Big Brother, Jesus, about how to be more loving.

More Rewards
- A pillar in God's Temple
- Name of God inscribed on you
- The City of God inscribed on you
- God's new Name inscribed on you

Jesus concludes:

He who overcomes, I will make him a pillar in the temple of My God, and he shall go out no more. I will write on him the name of My God and the name of the city of My God, the New Jerusalem, which comes down out of Heaven from My God. And I will write on him My new name. (Revelation 3:12)

Here's what I think it means to be a pillar for God. If you enjoyed being a pillar in an earthly church, just think of how great it will be to have this privilege in God's perfect church above. Being a pillar in God's temple doesn't mean that you will be stationary in a negative sense. There is probably an allusion here to the two pillars in the temple of Jerusalem, called Jachin and Boaz, meaning stability and strength. The Church is the temple; Christ is the foundation on which it is built; and his ministers are the Pillars by which, under him, it is adorned and supported.

"His name will be on their foreheads" (Revelation 22:4). Jesus' name represents what He is like and that we shall become more and more like Him without losing our own identity. His name also shows ownership. He knows who are His.

In God's Kingdom, we are not marked with a number like so many cattle, but we are sealed with Jesus' own dear name. We're sealed also with the name of the New Jerusalem—our homeland—and the Holy Spirit.... This is a threefold seal on our lives. What a sense of security this gives us! (Bennett, R., 1997, pp.153-154).

"He who has an ear, let him hear what the Spirit says to the churches" (Revelation 3:13).

Are you listening? Keep tuned in!

A Moment to Reflect and Pray

Take some time to discover the primary concepts that the Holy Spirit has quickened to you from this study of the church of Philadelphia. Write down the thoughts coming to you.

Are there any "crown stealers" in your life? What can you do to make yourself less vulnerable? To make yourself stronger? To be able to find spiritual swords in the Word more easily to refute the enemy's temptations?

Prayer

Dear Abba,

Thank You for sending Your dear Son to show me how to live like Him and the early Saints. Without You, Lord, I cannot live a strong biblical life-style. But with You I can do all things as I should.

I want my life to be pleasing to You as were those in Smyrna and Philadelphia. They were impressive Lord and an inspiration to me. How exciting it was for them to end up in Your Holy Word, the Bible, with not one criticism! Thanks for having the Apostle John write down all this exciting news for me to know about in this twenty-first century.

Increase my hunger for the Word, and fellowship with You in prayer. Help me make an impact on this world for good. Teach me how to love and to have a giving heart. May I remember to help the poor in the world: in Israel, Africa, and India. Anywhere you show me.

Teach me what Your plan is for my life, and help me be ready when Jesus comes—whether in life or in death.

I love and appreciate You so much! I delight in You—One God: Father, Son, and Holy Spirit.

Amen.

CHAPTER TWENTY

Invitation to the "Lukewarm" Church

Church of Laodicea

We've had an interesting journey to the seven churches of old Asia Minor, through the Book of Revelation. The seventh and concluding letter is to the church in wealthy Laodicea. Its location was about ninety miles east of Ephesus and twelve miles from Colossae. The city was renamed Laodicea in honor of the wife of Antiochus II (261-246 B.C.), not a positive family genealogy historically.

Conversely, the Apostle Paul was very instrumental in planting the gospel in the church of Laodicea. He mentions this connection in his epistle to the Colossians in which he greets them as brothers (Colossians. 2:1; 4:13).

The apostle Paul wrote the Laodiceans a letter but unfortunately, it was lost—perhaps in the eventual earthquake ruins of ancient Laodicea.

Revelation of Jesus Christ

The message, as in all previous letters, is from the Lord Jesus Christ:

> *And to the angel of the church of the Laodiceans write, "These things says the Amen, the Faithful and*

True Witness, the Beginning of the creation of God."
(Revelation 3:14)

- The Amen says
- The Faithful and True Witness
- Beginning of the creation of God

Earlier in Revelation, Jesus is described as "the Alpha and Omega" meaning "He is the first and last." Jesus "The Amen" to me reveals that, "He is the End; He brings finality to all earth's history."

The Faithful and True Witness: The word witness comes from martyr meaning faithful to speak the truth to your last breath—even if martyred in doing so. Jesus was the first martyr for what soon became known as Christianity.

The Beginning of the creation of God: The Lord Jesus, who was "eternally begotten of the Father," had no beginning (Guilbert, Nicene Creed, p. 358). Colossians 1:16-17 contains one of the major Scriptures that shows Jesus the Christ is eternal:

> *For by Him all things were created that are in Heaven and that are on earth, visible and invisible, whether thrones or dominions or principalities or powers. All things were created through Him and for Him. And He is before all things, and in Him all things consist.*

Yet when God the Son chose to come to earth as a baby, only in that sense did He have a beginning. Jesus, who is now in Heaven, still has a physical body though it is now mature and glorified.

Warning

Sadly, there was nothing to affirm in the church of Laodicea. *"I know your works, that you are neither cold nor hot. I could wish you were cold or hot"* (Revelation 3:15).

In the business world as a CEO, I find that the extremes do not work as well as a middle position. Thomas Kilman's *Conflict Mode Test* shows the value of different kinds of personalities. There are 5 types: competing, accommodating, avoiding, collaborating and compromising (Kilman, 1974, p. 8).

For example, the Speaker of the House in Congress needs to be able to compromise or a group will have a difficult time settling problems. The person with this gift can gracefully get out of destructive arguments. This person can arrive at a good solution under time pressure. A similar process can be seen in church business. The process will work with a pastor, church vestry, senior and junior warden.

However, what Jesus is speaking about here is in regards to one's faith. When it comes to faith in God there can be no compromises, lest one becomes a lukewarm compromiser in "Christianish" clothes.

There are bishops and clergy who in the last 30 years have written books against their own church's beliefs. For example, some have written against the Virgin Birth of Jesus. Some have written against the supernatural Resurrection of Jesus the Christ. Some have written against the virginity of Jesus and believe He was married to Mary Magdalene. Others have said that they do not believe Jesus' words: *"No man comes to the Father except through Me"* (John 14:6b).

Too often, they are not challenged by bishops and are allowed the right to continue to remain in leadership in the church. This is how the flock is led into a lukewarm belief system that Jesus expresses strong feelings about. A good thing to do to keep red hot is to write and challenge those who are writing to dilute the faith.

Warning Continues

The Son of God continues: *"So then, because you are lukewarm, and neither cold nor hot, I will vomit you out of*

My mouth" (Revelation 3:15). How graphic and clear can He get?

The Apostle Paul warns us, *"But know this, that in the last days perilous times will come.... [Men] having a form of godliness but denying its power. And from such people turn away!"* (2 Timothy 3:1,5).

The last days spoken of here began at Pentecost, and we've been in that season of time for 2,000 years now. Read all the verses in 2 Timothy, chapter 3 to see what Paul says these days will be like. A form of godliness may look impressive, but with no real belief there is no power.

Warning Continues

Jesus continues, *"Because you say, 'I am rich, have become wealthy, and have need of nothing'—and do not know that you are wretched, miserable, poor, blind, and naked...'"* (Revelation 3:17).

The church of Smyrna was actually "poor," but God called them "rich." They were not spiritually blind; their eyes were opened and anointed because they believed the Scriptures and lived them. They may have had old clothes on but they were getting ready to don the pure white linen robes of the saints. They may not have been wealthy on earth but they had beautiful homes being prepared for them in Heaven.

Jesus Gives Counsel
- Buy from Jesus refined gold
- Buy from Him white garments
- Buy from Him eye salve for sight

After Christ's serious challenge He gives an invitation:
I counsel you to buy from Me gold refined in the fire, that you may be rich; and white garments, that you may be clothed, that the shame of your nakedness may not

be revealed; and anoint your eyes with eye salve, that you may see. (Revelation 3:18)

In Isaiah 9:6, we see Jesus is named the "Wonderful Counselor." For those in the counseling field, as I am, it's important to counsel with human wisdom but it's even greater when the Holy Spirit is allowed to put His supernatural touch on the counseling session. We noticed in the Menorah Meditation in Chapter Eighteen, the third candle of the Isaiah Scripture highlighted the Spirit of Counsel.

Sometimes in life we have challenges that make us feel as though we've been burned and refined as gold in the fire. Jesus here is offering a gift of gold for truly He has been through the fire for you and me when He suffered the painful and humiliating death on the Cross.

He has prepared white garments of righteousness for us. He wants, as the Great High Priest, to take His anointing salve to touch our eyes so we will see visions and dreams and discernments in our walk with Him.

One night I had a dream that I had one eye that was open and one that was closed. As I awakened, puzzled, and prayed, about it I realized one eye was my Christian Gentile eye which was open, but the other was my Jewish eye which was closed. I hardly knew much about Jesus' life as a Jew or had any understanding about this part of my faith. I then understood that I could not see clearly unless I had sight for both eyes which encompassed my full vision, Judeo-Christian faith.

I also had a dream of Jesus walking through the churches in the Lampstand Menorah. Of course I did not know at that time I would be writing about the seven churches in this book.

Five Points Can Sum Up Mediocre Type Faith:
• Their life's goal is not "Thy Kingdom come" but "My Kingdom come."

• This church is "not hot or cold." That is, they were neither heathens nor Christians. If heathens, they might see their plight and change. Also they were listless and indifferent, not willing to stand and contend for their faith.

• The lukewarm lifestyle they exhibited was nauseating to God.

• Their viewpoint of themselves was full of pride and self-satisfaction: "I am rich. I have material goods. I need nothing." Perhaps this reflects their city that was a wealthy place with a famous medical school that produced a special eye salve, a rich banking center, and producer of famous black wool carpets.

• They were blind to their true spiritual condition. God's correction to them is: *"You are wretched, and miserable, and poor, and blind, and naked"* (Revelation 3:17b). Jesus is trying to shock them out of their worldly complacency, just as you might do with a rebellious, self-engrossed child.

Repent

His plaintive words as He calls to them are these: *"As many as I Love, I rebuke and chasten: be zealous therefore, and repent"* (Revelation 3:19).

"The people I love, I call to account —prod and correct and guide so that they'll live at their best. Up on your feet, then! About face! Run after God!" (Revelation 3:19, *The Message Bible*).

Repent (*metanoia*) means reversal of one's decision, reformation. (*Strong's*, Greek, e.g. Revelation 2:21, p.871, #3340, 41) Let's turn from our wrong direction. *"About face! Run after God."* He wants to be caught by you. He's hoping you'll love Him enough to chase after Him.

Reward

Behold, I stand at the door and knock. If anyone hears My voice and opens the door, I will come in to him and dine with him, and he with Me. (Revelation 3:20)

These very sad words to those who were once so close to Him are recorded for us. Here we see Jesus at the outside door of the church. They have closed their door to Him. Instead of Him being inside the door of their hearts, He is relegated to stand outside.

He calls to them: *"Behold, I stand at the door and knock: if anyone hears My voice, and opens the door, I will come into him. I will have Communion with him, and he with Me"* (Revelation 3:20, mod.). Can't you hear the love in His voice as He calls to them, through their closed door?

Is our own church lukewarm about their former love and zeal for the Lord Jesus Christ? Can we see ourselves in this church? Do we, too, need to repent? If Jesus stood at the door of our church and knocked, would anyone let Him in?

Witnessing at a Spa

Several months ago I was at a spa having a manicure. While my nails were drying a gentleman from Israel was waiting for his wife and struck up a conversation with me. We soon began to discuss writing books.

He said he wanted to write a book proving that there is no God. I took a deep breath and said that could be challenging. I said, "I do believe in God."

He responded, "If a man came to your door and said he is God, how would you know if he really is God?"

I was very surprised by his question but it did not take long for my answer. I said, "I would ask to see the nail prints in His hands." He looked at me thoughtfully for a bit and then changed the subject.

Jesus was knocking on his door that afternoon. I hope he won't forget the message. I did give him one of my recent *Edmond's Beacon* newspaper articles that had just been published.

For us individually, God cannot force open the door of our heart and spirit, even though He is greatest of all Loves. Neither could He do this for the congregants in the church of Laodicea or anyone else. Love does not force.

Reward Continues

To him who overcomes I will grant to sit with Me on My throne, as I also overcame and sat down with My Father on His throne. He who has an ear, let him hear what the Spirit says to the churches. (Revelation 3:21, 22)

• Sit with Christ on His throne in Heaven

Throne Privileges

In a previous chapter we discussed the awesome majesty of God's throne. Jesus is sitting with the Father on the throne to the Father's right; the thrones are as one, even as the Father and Son are one. And there in that scene you are welcomed. Jesus wants all the best for you.

When you experience a beautiful sunset, an inspiring song, or a lovely dinner, you want the person you love to experience that with you. In this greatest of honors, Jesus wants you beside Him. As faithful overcomers we will sit on that same throne. This means we will rule from this position of authority.

Paul's letter to the Ephesians shows us that spiritually we are seated in heavenly places right now due to our new birthright. But one day we will be there to see with our own eyes and experience all that it means to be invited to sit with Jesus on His glorious throne. What could be greater? (Bennett, R., *To Heaven and Back*, 1997, p.154).

Leading a Child in Prayer

At a meeting some years ago, a six year-old girl brought her five year-old friend, Susie (I'll call her) to me for prayer. The purpose was that she wanted to accept Jesus.

I said, "Susie, your heart is like a door and Jesus is standing outside wanting to come in and bring you wonderful gifts of eternal life, love, peace, joy, beautiful songs, poetry. Does that sound good, Susie?"

"Yes, Ma'am it does."

"Well, God has made your heart with the door-handle on the inside because He never forces people to love Him. He patiently waits for you to choose to open the door. Would you like to invite Him in, Susie?"

"Oh yes, I would."

"The next thing is for you to do is to invite Him in. Just say, 'Come in Jesus.'"

She closed her eyes, folded her hands and said, "Come on in, Jesus."

We waited. I said, "Did He come in Susie?"

She said, "I still hear Him knocking."

I waited.

Then she said, "Oh yes, He's here, in my heart!"

This was not just a creative game but I believe Jesus accepted that invitation. In fact,

I heard from the parents years later and their daughter is still a committed Christian.

Whoever Will May Come

This was applying Revelation 3:20 to a five year-old.

With an older person you could have him read the verse aloud, and then help him pray. You could also add John 3:16 as your first Scripture reference and perhaps another favorite.

Since you've read this *Heaven Tours* book, you know many of the other spiritual helps I've suggested for one's spiritual direction.

It is wonderful when you and I can help others to make that simple, yet eternally important step into God's Kingdom. God has made salvation a simple process so that anyone can come into the Family of God.

A Moment to Reflect and Pray

By reading these chapters about the seven churches, you have also read and pondered all the final words of Jesus sent directly from Heaven to the body of Christ via John the Apostle. I believe our Lord is pleased that you did this. All His words are in italics so they will stand out for you.

Take a few minutes to think about this and see what you might want to journal.

Will you check your spiritual inner door and see if the Lover of your soul is standing there waiting for an invitation to come in, or to come back in, or to have more fellowship with you?

Be sure to invite Him in to have fellowship with you. Tell Him all you've been wanting to say. Pour out your love to Him. Let tears come. Do not hold them back. He loves you so much! He believes in you. He wants to help you carry any burdens. He will lead you to answers in His Word and through His seasoned leaders who are biblically sound. You're on the way to a new growth period. Thanks be to God!

Prayer

Dear Father God, I want to be a Soul Winner for You and Your Son. When I get to Heaven I want to see others whom I helped invite into the Kingdom. Empower me with the Holy Spirit, fill me with your Word and give me a love for those who do not know You.

Thank you for giving me this ministry of Reconciliation. *"Now ... God has reconciled me to Himself through Jesus Christ ... He's committed to me the word of reconciliation"* (2 Corinthians 5:18-20, personalized). May I be like *"those who turn many to righteousness"* (Daniel 12:3b).

Help me to never be a lukewarm believer, but one filled with your Holy Fire, Power, and Love.

In Jesus' redeeming name,

Amen.

Heaven's Awards Surpass All Others

Overcomers Include You

Let us consider the exciting message God gives to spiritual overcomers. For seven chapters we've studied the seven churches from the final book of the Bible, Revelation.

In review they are:

- Ephesus the church in danger of leaving her first love;
- Smyrna the church who was persecuted for her strong faith;
- Pergamus the compromising church;
- Thyatira the church with good works, but short on the Word.
- Sardis the church that needs Holy Spirit Reviving;
- Philadelphia the brotherly loving church; and
- Laodicea the lukewarm church.

A message to each church was given by the resurrected Jesus, in Heaven, through His beloved Apostle John. John was caught up from earth to the Lord's throne in a visionary or Near-Death experience (Revelation 1:10, 11).

These seven ancient churches of Asia Minor *represent your church and my church today.* We have looked at the messages that clearly and emphatically give us information about what God does and does not like!

In each of these seven letters, Jesus ends with a message to "Those Who Overcome." Each time He also repeats, *"He who has an ear to hear, let him hear what the Spirit says to the churches."*

You would think after a repetition of seven times, we human beings might take notice! We have learned that there were overcomers as well as unbelievers in the seven churches.

Jesus gives to each church part of the description of the *Eternal Awards Ceremony* coming in Heaven. This goes beyond achieving Medals in the Olympic Games or the Hollywood Oscar awards, as those only last for this life.

Heaven's Awards add up to thirteen prepared for earth's Overcomers.

• **The tree of life**—The first human couple had to be removed from the *Garden of Eden* to be kept from eating from the Tree of Life while in a fallen state. Now in Heaven, there is no limit to the feast.

• **Crown of life**—An un-forfeitable possession at the end of life. Usually seen as being given to Martyrs for Christ. There are four other crowns for us in the New Testament. They are: Watcher's Crown (Crown of Righteousness), Soul Winner's Crown (Crown of Rejoicing), Crown of Purity (Incorruptible Crown), and Shepherd's Crown (Crown of Glory).

• **Escape from the second death**—This is an escape from spiritual death. The Overcomer may die physically, but he or she will never die spiritually.

• **Hidden manna**—Biblically this refers to Israel being fed in the wilderness. A pot of manna was preserved in the Ark of the Covenant. The "hidden manna" can be spiritual food for us from the Ark in Heaven.

• **A white stone and a new name**—In ancient times a white stone was used for admission to all public festivals. Believers will be admitted to Messiah's Wedding Feast. What is the new name? My guess is "Bride of Christ." However, "a new name" is His surprise.

• **Reigning with Christ**—This speaks of the defeat of earth's rebelliousness, when Christ will reign. Also an answer to The Lord's Prayer, "Thy Kingdom come."

• **The Bright and Morning Star**—A title for Jesus Christ who is the greatest Gift (Revelation 22:16).

• **Walking with Christ, in White Garments**—This is beyond *Walking with God in the cool of the day in the Garden of Eden,* as this time it is without end.

• **Name eternally in the Book of Life**—What confidence this gives us!

• **Confession of your name before Father God and His angels**—Awesome! We also need to confess our Savior's Name before persons on earth to confirm this promise to us (Matthew 10:32).

• **Pillar of honor in God's temple**—This is a symbol of eternal abiding with God.

• **Written upon you will be:** God's name, Heaven's New Jerusalem name, and Christ's new name—My guess for Christ's new name is: *Yishi* (Hebrew) meaning "Husband." Christ finally has His Bride, the name given for all believers. He had no physical Bride on earth, though we are presently betrothed to Him, through faith.

• **Seated with Christ on His Throne**—Even now, believers are "spiritually" seated with Him in heavenly places (Ephesians 2:6). There is no greater place than this: to at last be seated with the Son of God, on His Throne in Heaven.

Together we have taken time to study our Lord Jesus' last written message to us from Heaven, until He comes. Let us get ready for Heaven's Awards Ceremony—it's the ultimate! And if you so choose … the winner is … You!

Heavenly Postlude

" The Church is for more than hatching, matching, and dispatching," said Dennis Bennett, with a smile.

I agreed with him, smiling back. This was my one of my late husband's favorite quips.

It is very important to have the Church at the beginning, middle, and ending of life, but there is more for the Christian journey than that. For instance, I'd like to see more "Teaching Churches" where the members have opportunities to do more than surfing over the Bible, but can get into the waters deeply and even scuba dive to observe the depths of God's wonders.

As the messages to the Churches in Revelation have shown us, our Lord is not happy with churches where a kind of Nicolaitan oversight does its best to curtail those who are wanting to develop into biblical, Holy Spirit inspired leaders. And not everyone has a "ministerial call" or can afford to go to seminary, yet development for service can begin right at the home church and go out to our world to share the Gospel—the Good News.

I'd like to see more churches that are "Teaching Churches" manned by laity "Teaching Teams" who volunteer to serve their Lord this way. After all, there are 66 books of the Bible. Each of us has only one life, to study and to share these Books of Wisdom that guide us all on how to live. We are privileged to be people of The Book.

How many books of the Bible have we been taught thus far? Are we ready to teach our children, our neighbors? No matter how many degrees you and I have, we are not fully educated unless we are students growing in wisdom and knowledge of God's bestseller, the Bible.

In my Dream Church, beyond the important and basic Sunday School, on varying levels, I would have seminars in:

• The Motivational Gifts, The Spiritual Gifts, The Lord's Prayer, How to be Emotionally Free, How to Study the Bible, Intercessory Prayer, Basic Hebrew and our Judeo-Christian Heritage, The Value of Holy Communion, How to be an Empowered Leader, The Ten Commandments, Basic Greek for the New Testament

• Applying the Beatitudes, How to have a Successful Marriage, Communication Skills for Couples, Premarital Skills for Young Adults, Whole Armor of God Prayer, Nutrition for the Family, Dad's Leading Family Meditations, Using Banners in Creative Dance, Hebraic Dance, Touring Heaven Through the Bible, Healing Grief from Loss

• The Books of John, Matthew, Acts of the Apostles, the Epistles, Books of Moses, Revelation, and any and all Books of the Bible.

Depending on the size of the church, at least several of these topics, or others, can eventually be chosen and taught at the same time. What an exciting hub of activity and growth there can be.

Missionary Teaching Outreaach

A Church or Organization can also do missionary outreach. For example, since 1999 the course, *Emotionally Free® for East Africa* has been translated into the Kiswahili language, *Uhura wa Kihisia*. Sharing of Ministries Abroad (SOMA-USA) in conjunction with Christian Renewal Association, Inc. (CRA) has developed the African Basic Syllabus.

This East African project was spearheaded by Gail Patton, *Emotionally Free®* Teacher and SOMA missionary, and directed by Edwina Thomas, SOMA-USA National Director,

Woodbridge, VA 22193. What wonderful healings and miracles have happened through their powerful ministry.

The second edition of the, *Emotionally Free® Course, South African Edition* is completing translation in *Setswana* proposed for 2009. The Rev. Michael Messina, Rector and missionary is working with CRA, SOMA and Gail Patton on this project.

The *Emotionally Free®* course officially began in the USA in 1980 as I had developed and copyrighted it. Check our CRA web site for more valuable information and teaching locations in America, and other countries (www.EmotionallyFree.org).

I studied with *Bible Study Fellowship* for seven years following my widowhood in 1991, and have notebooks on much of the Bible in my library. It was a great study. I agree with them on nearly one hundred percent of their teaching.

My favorite thing is using View Binder Notebooks to save all my learning in. There are also excellent Radio Bible Studies with notes to print off from your computer.

Kay Arthur's Course, *Revelation Inductive—Precept Bible Study,* and her radio program are enriching. I recommend her *Daniel Inductive* study also. These two books, Revelation and Daniel, are important for all Believers to study in this 21st Century. I like to stay flexible on pre- or mid-tribulation viewpoints and let the Holy Spirit guide me personally.

Bible Language Translation Grows

Jewish Scribes spent their entire lives hand copying the Hebrew *Torah* (*Pentatuke* Gr.). Christian Bible Scholars translated the Bible into English at the threat of death. It took Johann Gutenberg in 1455 with the first printing press, to print the first Bible, *Biblia Latina.*

In 1526, the New Testament was translated from Greek to English, by scholar and martyr, William Tyndale. In 1535, Old and New Testaments were translated into English by Myles

Coverdale reprinted from the copy in the Library of the Duke of Sussex.

In 1611, the *Authorized King James Version of the Bible* was executed by order of King James 1st, completed and published that year. From there on, a Bible language translation explosion took place. (See *American Bible Society* online.)

"The Bible continues to be the most translated book in the world ... The Bible is available in whole or in part to some 98 percent of the world's population in a language in which they are fluent" (*Wikipedia Foundation, Inc.* 11/28/08).

To me the most important mission of "the Church," is being equipped to do the work we've been put on the planet to do. Know God, know His Word, and effectively tell others about Him.

A Starting Point

In chapter two of this book, I told how *A Heavenly Beginning Shaped my Life*. If my mother, Loretta Reed, had not had a Death and Return Experience while giving birth to me, and told me about it in my childhood, I might not have been predisposed to write several books and a syllabus about Heaven. I didn't realize until later in my life that I would have a calling to write on this subject.

One of the starting points for me in doing so was the sudden death of my husband, Dennis Bennett, in 1991. In his childhood, while still living in England, he was quarantined a month with rheumatic fever. In his late sixties it caught up with him while we were traveling in ministry. He contracted the Asian flu, and it hit his weakest point—his heart valve—and the murmur returned. Dennis was a man of faith and decided he did not want surgery for a prolapsed heart valve. Seven years later, at age 74, he died while writing at his computer.

Dennis was an Episcopal priest whose goal was not to build a denomination, or a parish church, or an organization, but rather to build the Kingdom of God. His ministry was therefore strongly ecumenical.

Several historical books honored him after his death: *The 100 Most Important Events in Christian History* (Curtis, Lang, Peterson; 1991, pp. 197,198), and *The Century of the Holy Spirit* (Synan, 2001, pp. 8,151-153).

Dennis and I had walked hand-in-hand in ministry for our 25 years of marriage. I missed him greatly. After a year and nine months, I regained my direction and continued our ministry as president and CEO of Christian Renewal Association, Inc.

Researching Heaven

My serious research on Heaven began. I kept running into people who had Near-Death Experiences. You know that interested me intensely and was very healing. After meeting seven people who had NDE's, it seemed the Holy Spirit was leading me to write a book that became *To Heaven and Back* published in 1997. This was the first biblical, Christian NDE book on the market. The pictures on my web site and now in this new book *Heaven Tours* grew out of that first book.

Before long, life brought me into awareness of eight more supernatural experiences of friends I had known, and some of those life messages evolved before my eyes. Some I gleaned by talking specifically about this book as I was writing it, which brought out experiences I had never heard before. Two of the eight people were discovered through friends. I elaborated on the ninth story, my mother's story, in more detail than ever before.

This time not all are NDE testimonies but some are heavenly death experiences. To this book two other new gifts were added, that is, the illustrations of Heaven that were developed following *To Heaven and Back*, and the newly published chapters in *Part Two—Jesus' Latest Words from Heaven*. These are the Messages of Jesus to the Seven Churches of Revelation, and to You.

Faith in God through His Son who conquered death gives Believers less fear at the time of death. The Apostle Paul said, *"The last enemy that will be destroyed is death"* (1 Corinthians 15:26). Jesus died on the Jewish Passover Feast, and He was raised from the dead three days later on the Feast of First Fruits. Because He was raised from death, He promises those who believe in Him and His words will also be raised.

At Death, We Will Not Be Alone

In 2006, I received an email from a woman who said, "I have a bit of a hang-up on death. However, I know that I am saved and will live eternally with my Lord and Savior." Lauren continued, "I was told something helpful yesterday by a business friend of mine: 'When we die, we will not be alone because Christ's omnipresence is still with us. Death is a peaceful experience and not anything to be afraid of.'

"Well, today I went to Google.com and typed in 'Pictures of Heaven' and your web site came up. As I was looking at your pictures, tears streamed down my face. How wonderfully you have depicted what I have read from the Bible!

"So to make a long story short, thank you for following your calling with your beautiful pictures and beautiful words. May God bless you even more to allow a bigger 'glimpse' of Heaven to shine from your web site. You turned words into pictures! From Lauren."

Words like these make the bumps on the road of life insignificant to me.

Heaven Tours

I began these true stories of Heaven with the experience of my mother. You will remember her poem in chapter two where she talked about meeting Jesus, the Crimson Rose of Sharon, and that each of her children will meet her on that pathway of fragrant roses. She had no idea about how her poem would bless me and that it would go out to you reading this, and bring you the fragrance of Christ.

I, too, have written a poem that I'll leave with you.

Heaven — Be There

Heaven, do I dare
Believe in you
A place prepared
A Home for those
Who love God

Who are the witnesses
I can believe
Those who lived
Before me
Whose word I can trust

Heaven, please be there
When I need you

Some, like Lazarus
Jesus' friend, went
And came back
Only to die again

And Paul visited
Saw and heard mysteries
Came back, and died
As a martyr in Rome

Some I've met, and
Even my mother,
Took a wonderful trip
A few of them have already
Died and others live on
For now

All are grand
Encouraging confirmations

But who has died
Was raised from the dead
In a transformed body
Went to Heaven
Came back for 40 days
Then left with a promise

"I'll be back for you"[21]

Only One
Jesus Christ

One whose
Witness is first
And is more than
Enough
For us all

Your Home
    The Bible says a mansion—a home—has been prepared for you. It will be exactly what you need, built by the One who created the universe. Your family and friends will know where

you are located. All you've lost will be restored to you. Perhaps even your dear pets will be there.

The fragrances are of the incense which are the collected prayers of the saints, and of Christ's own presence: myrrh, frankincense, aloes, and cassia. Fragrance of flowers fill the air: roses, lilies, honeysuckle, lavender, plumaria, orange blossoms, blended fragrances from the many fruit trees, and more.

Music, singing, and dancing are everywhere. People are dancing on the golden streets or the wide jasper walls. There is so much to rejoice over: no more sickness, or pain, or parting, or losses, or disappointment, or abuse, or emptiness.

We're with God who loves us beyond all loves. We've been invited to God's everlasting party.

Greatest Moments Ahead

Stop for a moment, close your eyes, and take a deep breath of hope. Picture yourself there with your loved ones greeting you. Notice the angels welcoming you. See your name in the Lamb's book of life. Notice the Welcome Home message at the top of the Pearl Gate.

The tunnel of light is drawing you inside with your friends cheering you on. You are entering into the greatest praise-a-thon you have ever seen. The light from the Throne though hundreds of miles away is brightly but gently shining on you. Pain has left your body.

You're thinking, "Oh—I want to see Jesus; He is the One who made it possible to have eternal life." You take off running down the streets of gold and leaping for joy as you go. Your spirit body is so light that you feel like you're in outer space.

You're thinking, "Oh—I also want to see Father God who sent His Son to pay the debt for my sins. Through Jesus He has become my Father too. Oh Father, I long to see You too."

You pick a delicious piece of fruit off the tree and taste heavenly fruit that is like twelve kinds of fruit blended into one. It not only tastes good it energizes you for the journey.

Fully satisfied you continue on your pilgrimage to the center of Heaven and the Throne of God.

As you go you think, "Oh—I want to experience the Holy Spirit, He is the One who as a heavenly Matchmaker, pursued me and drew me to understand about the Heavenly Bridegroom seeking for a Bride. He helped me understand Scripture so that I could comprehend the mysteries of God more clearly."

You take a dip into the River of Life and swim for more refreshment. The experience is beyond description. Others are doing the same. You eventually lie on the grass in the Garden of Eden location and feel total peace. You recognize the sweet Comforter, the presence of the Holy Spirit and thank Him. He is there all around you.

Again you remember there is a place a Home prepared for you and are greeted by an angel. He tells you about your new home. You run along together until you stand before the Throne of God with a joyful throng of Saints. Your loved ones gather around you.

Jesus makes His way to you, welcomes you Home and embraces you. You feel all the love you ever experienced on earth rolled into one, in His arms. When He says, "I love you," you swoon and He holds you up. In time you find yourself on His arm, as He proudly takes you up the stairs to His Father and your Father too.

You meet Father God face to face and now you have a perfect Father who will show you what a true Father's love is. He says, "My child I have been waiting for you. You are Home."

Father and Jesus hold you in a circle of their love as you say the words: "*Abba, Abba* Father. Daddy, Daddy, I love you. Jesus, Jesus, *Yeshua*, my Savior, I love You."

The presence of the dove-like Holy Spirit anoints you from the top of your head to the toes of your feet. You sway under the anointing and are held up by angel's wings. The power of the Holy Comforter is truly here and is that familiar feeling known on earth, only greater.

Yes, it is better than you'd ever dreamed and the eternal adventure is just beginning. There is much to get ready for: the Awards Ceremony, Marriage Supper of the Lamb, Preparation to bring the Kingdom to Earth-as-it-is-in-Heaven. It is a Kingdom, an adventure without end.

There I leave you on your journey. You've had the beginning of your *Heaven Tours* even now while still on earth, and in the Kingdom above you will have *Heaven Without End.* It begins on earth and continues one glorious day in God's Heavenly City.

Amen and Amen.

Invitation to
Eternal Life Extravaganza

Dear Friend, you do not want to miss this Eternal Life Extravaganza. Right now, set your heart on this forever goal. Write your name and date in your Bible at Revelation 22:17 to answer this invitation sent from the heavenly Bridegroom, Jesus, through the Holy Spirit. Tell someone you said, "Yes, I'm coming."

> *The Spirit and the Bride say, Come.*
> *And let him that hears say, Come.*
> *And let him that is thirsty come.*
> *And whosoever will, let him, let her*
> *take the water of life freely.*

Endnotes

1 Rita Bennett, *To Heaven and Back* (Grand Rapids, MI: Zondervan, 1997) p.18.

2 Melvin Morse and Paul J. Perry, *Transformed by the Light* (New York: Villard/Random, 1992), ix-xiii.

3 The treatment for diabetes was discovered at the University of Toronto Medical School, Dr. Fredrick Banting is usually mentioned as a primary person for this feat. See: About Diabetes.com: Inventions online, November 30, 2007.

4 Matthew Henry, *Matthew Henry's Commentary in One Volume* (Grand Rapids, MI: Zondervan Publishing, 1961), p. 1,985. Commentator Matthew Henry notes this about the gates and those who will enter: "As the city had four equal sides, answering to the four quarters of the world, so on each side there were three gates, signifying that there is as free an entrance from one part of the world as from the other." Another great thought.

5 In the e-mail from Merla Watson, she is quoting a Rabbi friend in Jerusalem, March 17, 2002, and she has given me permission to quote from her e-mail.

6 See footnotes about believers being the pearl of great price that Jesus gives His all to buy. The *Schofield Reference Edition of the Bible*, Rev. C.I. Schofield, D.D. (New York: Oxford University Press) p. 1017.

7 A believing Jew here refers to the early followers of Jesus who were mainly Jews as *Yeshua* came "first to the Jews." They were of the race He, the Son of God, chose to be born into. It can also refer to Jews who died believing, and those who are presently and in the future, looking for Messiah to return to earth.

8   Other biblical names for Heaven are: *The Father's house;
A City with Foundations; A better Country; City of the
Living God; Enduring City, The New Jerusalem, The Holy
City, Jerusalem; The dwelling of God; The bride, the wife
of the Lamb* (John 14:2; Hebrews 11:10; Hebrews 11:15,16;
Hebrews 12:22; Hebrews 13:14; Revelation 21:2; Revelation
21:2,10;22:19; Revelation 21:3; Revelation 21:9).

9   *Seattle Public Library* quick information.

10 Ibid.

11 Rita Bennett, *To Heaven and Back* (Grand Rapids, MI:
Zondervan Publishing, 1997), p. 200.

12 For Sally we've chosen to use the term *Death and Return
Experience* (D&RE) in this true story to describe one who has
died, and come back after having a supernatural touch from
God. To some, the well-known term Near-Death Experience
can be confusing as it sounds as though the person did not die
since, after all, they came back. When a person has ceased to
breathe for over 4 or 5 minutes, it can be said they have died.
This term, *Death and Return Experience,* was used first in my
book *To Heaven and Back* in Dr. Gerard Landry's thrilling
story. He preferred that term also.

13 Shade O'Driscoll's Story—Addendum: *Welcoming a New Life.*
After returning to Seattle from Jan's funeral, there were still
days of sadness and tears, but God had a wonderful gift on the
way for me and my family, Baby Tristan. A month earlier I had
witnessed the last hours of one life leaving this earth, and now I
was about to witness the first moments of another life arriving.
Joanna, our youngest daughter was expecting her second child
the first week of December. She requested that I be there with
her husband during the birthing as a *doula* (one who assists
with the birth).
How precious is life! Holding the baby, Tristan in my arms
seconds after his first breath, looking into that dear little face
that was known and planned in the womb of Father's heart was
surely witnessing a miracle, the miracle of life.
I knew his little spirit was there as he responded to the love in
my voice. My spirit bonded with his as I welcomed him into
this world, into our family, and the family of God. Jeremiah 1:5
tells us that Father God knew Tristan and ordained his place

on this earth before he was ever formed in his mother's womb. Thus his origin was God's heart of love. Life comes from God; it is a sacred trust to hold, both our own life and the lives of those entrusted to us.

Filled with Joy: Joanna chose not to have medication during Tristan's birth. At times the pain was very great, and she had to push very hard to bring her little son into the world. Jesus chose to birth us into the Kingdom of God by taking our sins into His own body through the terrible pain of crucifixion. When Joanna held her baby, joy filled her heart, the pain was forgotten. Hebrews 12:2 tells us, Jesus for the joy that was set before Him endured the cross. We are the Lord's joy, He endured the cross for us that we might live with Him forever in Heaven. Thanks be to God for His great gift of life on this earth and life eternal. Amen.

14 *The Interlinear Greek-English New Testament* by translator, The Reverend Alfred Marshall D.Litt., publisher Samuel Bagster and Sons Limited, London, 1964.

15 *The New Unger's Bible Dictionary* by Merrill F. Unger, Editor R.K. Harrison, The Moody Bible Institute of Chicago Publisher, 1957 – 1988.

16 *The Spirit-Filled Life Bible* says, the altar of Zeus was 200 ft. tall.

17 Ibid., p. 986.

18 www.truthablaze.com/pergamos, 9-15-08.

19 Harvard and Cornell Universities have sponsored annual archeological expeditions to Sardis since 1958 (Columbia University Press on-line.) *The Zondervan Pictorial Bible Dictionary*, p. 754.

20 To understand Revelation 3:9, read Stern's *Jewish New Testament Commentary* page 796. To grasp this first century verse, and others, we must read them with early Christian and Jewish insight.

21 In Rita Bennett's poem, *Heaven—Be There*, The quote of Jesus saying, "I'll be back for you" is from John 14:3 (KJV, mod).

References

Baltsan, Hayim, author, (1991). *Webster's New World Hebrew Dictionary.* New York: Simon and Schuster.

Barnhart, David R., author, (2007). *Living in the Times of the Signs.* Florida: Xulon Press.

Bennett, Rita M. M.A. (1997). *To Heaven and Back: True Stories of those who Have Made the Journey.* Michigan: Zondervan (A Division of Harper Collins).

Church, J.R. Dr., Editor, (September, 2007). *Prophecy in the News Magazine: Rosh Hashanah 5768 A Sabbatical Year!.* Oklahoma City: Prophecy in the News.

Clarke, Adam LL.D., born Ireland (1801/1825). *Clarke's Commentary*, Vol 5. Nashville, Abingdon.

Cornwall, Judson Rev. (1989). *Heaven.* Florida: Bridge-Logos.

Dake, Finis Jennngs, Rev. (1963). *Dake's Annotated Reference Bible.* Georgia, Dake Bible Sales.

Guilbert, Charles Mortimer, Custodian of the book, (1979). *The Book of Common Prayer*. New York: Oxford University Press.

Hayford, Jack W., B.A., D.D. Litt.D. (1991). *Spirit-Filled Life Bible*. Nashville: Thomas Nelson.

Henry, Matthew, The Reverend, D.D. (1961). *Matthew Henry's Commentary in One Volume*. Michigan: Zondervan.

Kilmann, Ralph H., (1974). *Thomas-Kilmann Conflict Mode Instrument*. New York: Xicom Incorporated.

Kolenberger lll, John R. (1979-1987). *The Interlinear NIV Hebrew-English Old Testament*. Michigan: Zondervan Publishing House.

Levitt, Zola (1979). *The Seven Feasts of Israel*. Texas (Dallas): Box 12268.

Marshall, Alfred, The Reverend, D. Litt. (1958-1964). *The Interlinear Greek-English New Testament*. London: Samuel Bagster and Sons Ltd.

Morse, Melvin, M.D. and Perry, Paul J. (1992). *Transformed by the Light*. New York: Villard/Random.

Nuland, Sherwin, M.D. (1993). *How We Die*. New York: Vintage Books.

Rothblum, Bergman, and Band, (1987). *Hebrew Primer.* New Jersey: Behrman House.

Schlessinger, Dr. Laura and Rabbi S. Vogel, (1998). *The Ten Commandments: Significance of God's Laws in Everyday Life.* New York: HarperCollins.

Sommerville, Robert (2008). *Lamp of God–Menorah: What Christians Should Know About It.* Alabama: Awareness Ministry.

Stachorek, Gerrish and Wheatley, (2008). *Untying Israel's Tongue.* www.Israelmybeloved.com.

Stern, David H. Ph.D., M.Div., (1998). *Complete Jewish Bible.* Maryland: Jewish New Testament.

Strong, James LL.D., (1984). *The New Strong's Exhaustive Concordance of the Bible.* Nashville, Thomas Nelson.

Tenny, Merrill C. Gen. Editor, Ph.D. Harvard U., (1963-1971). *The Zondervan Pictorial Bible Dictionary.* Michigan: Zondervan.

Unger, Merrill Frederick, Ph.D., D. Semitics, (1957,1988). *The New Unger's Bible Dictionary.* Chicago: The Moody Bible Institute.

WHAT PEOPLE HAVE SAID ABOUT THE
HEAVEN TOURS WEB SITE

Feedback From
www.EmotionallyFree.com

Having read the book, *To Heaven and Back,* I was so happy to see the pictures!! I plan to share the web site with friends in Christ here in Bozeman.
– Thyrza Z., 12/15/00, Montana.

[Note: The illustrations that developed from my first book on Heaven were then placed on my web site, and now are included here in *Heaven Tours* as a first publication. – Rita Bennett]

What a wonderful blessing to be able to view the pictures on my computer and get a glimpse of what Heaven will be like. I lost my husband to cancer in 1995 and learning about what Heaven is like comforts me to know where my precious husband is living. We attended Carl Strader's church in Lakeland and he gave me Ms. Springer's book on Heaven and today Joyce Strader called to tell me about your web site and your book. God bless you for all the work you have done to prepare these pictures and scriptures for us to enjoy and study. In His Wonderful, Matchless Love, I am His Forever,
– Helen R.U., 12/16/00, Florida.

As for your Web site on Heaven, it is great! I know I need to have permission to print the pictures, but I was so impressed with *The Majestic Throne of God* that I printed it for my

personal prayer time. I hope it was all right? Again my sole purpose will be for my personal use. Thanks for response.
    – Steve S., 12/3/00, Massachusetts.

    I am undone. About to let go the tears I am holding back. In awe of what God has led you to accomplish as teacher and comforter to those invested in Heaven, the Kingdom of Our Lord. I am in awe. What more can I say? I am grateful to God that He has provided for us to be in this company of believers on earth and in Heaven. Much love to you all,
    – Lois M., 10/17/00, Oregon.

    I was surfing and found your name in the TBN address book. I have never heard about your name and ministries. I have never seen this before and I was truly touched! I'm going to try and get some of your materials. What a trip I took tonight! I was so thrilled and excited to see these drawings. I hope I can dream of something like this. It is worth it to serve our Lord and Savior. It is worth going through all of this because we do have a place in Heaven and to see our MASTER! Oh, how wonderful and beautiful it must be. I'm going to tell my friends and loved ones about this web site.
    – Rosalie J., 10/05/00.

    Beautiful … I wept seeing what I had only pictured in my mind while reading Revelation. I wept also knowing so many loved ones have gone through the gate. Blessed be His Holy Name!
    – Ann R., Pastor's wife, 9/22/00.

    Friday night I took my mother to dinner and brought her home to look at the Heaven Tour. She is 76 and is going through that stage in her life where she has as many friends in Heaven as on earth. It was such a comfort!
    – Montie R., 9/26/00, Montana.

My 5-year old son is always pestering me with questions about Heaven—where is it? What does it look like? etc. etc. as only a 5-year old can ... (Now) I can finally show my son just a hint of what we have to look forward to some day. It was so wonderful! He really got excited and said he couldn't wait to get there. He wanted to know if we could eat the fruit of the trees and if it would taste good! Thanks so much for doing the work to put this together. I know God is in it.
– Lauren S., 2000.

I was able to check out most of your web site. Didn't have time today to read all the info on the Heaven Tour, but the pictures are wonderful!! I guess I had no idea how extensive that work has been with all the research and writing. I am impressed! Wow! Thank you for being faithful to what God has called you to do and for taking time to stay current with the latest technology.
– Dianne H., 2000, Washington State.

This was completely awesome—cannot express how beautifully God has used your research for the Kingdom of God. God bless you mightily ... I've sat with tears in my eyes— when one thinks of Heaven and how we need to be ready so that we may enter that wonderful place—the things of this earth do grow strangely dim.
– Carol B., 2000.

It's amazing! I was so excited I showed everyone at church and they were astonished to actually picture Heaven. Our pastor is very practical in his teaching. I just could not focus on God's Word even though I read it a lot, but these pictures keep me concentrating on God. You are a real blessing and a miracle. Love,
– Cathy, 2/29/00 Washington State.

Thank you for the glimpse of Heaven ... I'll see you there.
    – Shirley K., 3/1/00.

Recommended Books

Heaven Titles

Bennett, Rita (1997). *To Heaven and Back.* Grand Rapids, MI: Zondervan.

This is Rita's first book on Heaven which sold over 200,000 copies. It is the first Christian book on Near-Death experiences. Seven NDE true stories begin the book; the second half is an inspiring, comprehensive biblical picture of Heaven. Now available through *Christian Renewal Association, Inc.* (425) 775-1768. www.EmotionallyFree. org

Bennett, Rita (2009). *Heaven Tours.* Alachua, FL: Bridge-Logos Publishing.

Rita's second book on Heaven is the one you are reading, or hopefully will read. This time she's writing not only on Near-Death Experience examples but a mixture of NDES, one time Heaven trips, and Jesus' final words sent from Heaven to the Church - past and present.

Rita's web site Tour Pictures and Commentary evolved out of writing *To Heaven and Back.* Now for the first time you can see the pictures that were only spoken of in her earlier book. The illustrations in *Heaven Tours,* take the reader on his or her own personal tour

Cornwall, Judson (1989). *Heaven*. Alachua, FL: Bridge-Logos Publishing.

Here you will experience comprehensive biblical teaching on Heaven by a well-seasoned and treasured pastor who is now rejoicing in the fuller Kingdom above.

Kreeft, Peter (1989). *Heaven*. San Francisco, CA: Ignatius Press.

Rita learned about this book by reading Joni Eareckson-Tada's book *Heaven: Your Real Home.* It is beautifully and poetically written.

Lewis, C.S. (1946). *The Great Divorce*. New York, NY: Macmillan.

This is a fiction story of a spiritual bus ride from the outskirts of hell to the outskirts of Heaven and the reasons why some chose to stay, and others did not. This book is a favorite of Rita's.

Lewis, C.S. (1988). *A Grief Observed*. New York, NY: Macmillan.

Dr. Lewis walks us through the battles he fought to rediscover his faith after the death of his wife. This masterpiece has comforted beyond thousands.

Lewis, C.S. (1956). *The Last Battle*. New York, NY: Macmillan.

This fictional story is the last book in the Chronicles of Narnia series. Adventures lead the reader to the realization that the lowly stable is the way into Heaven. It concludes with a beautiful description of "God's Country."

Piper, Don (2004). *90 Minutes in Heaven:* Grand Rapids, MI: Fleming H. Revell.

Karen Grafton of Orlando, Florida wrote to Rita, October 30, 2005: "If we were to be told to evacuate because of a dangerous oncoming hurricane, the first things I would pack up to take with us would be all my Bibles, and my collection of true testimonies of Heaven. Your book, 'To Heaven and Back' and Don Piper's book '90 Minutes in Heaven' are in that category."

Karen enclosed a copy of Rev. Don Piper's book encouraging Rita to read his Heaven experience on pages 21 through 36. Rita Bennett continues to recommend "his powerful book."

Sauvage, Lester R. (1996). *The Open Heart.* Deerfield Beach, FL: Health Communications, Inc.

A world-renowned heart surgeon tells the moving stories of ten of his patients who went to the brink of death. Each came through coronary bypass surgery with renewed purpose.

Springer, Rebecca (1995 reprint). *Within the Gates* (1995). Dallas, TX: Christ for the Nations.

Reasons for the longevity of this more than 80-year old book are revealed when you read about Rebecca's coma and her four-day vision of Heaven. This is a quick and easy read.

Eareckson-Tada, Joni (1995). *Heaven: Your Real Home.* Grand Rapids, MI: Zondervan.

As Joni is an artist on canvas, she is also an artist with words. Here she verbally paints a pathway to Heaven's door.

OTHER SUBJECTS

Bennett, Rita (1982). *You Can Be Emotionally Free.* Alachua, FL: Bridge-Logos Publishing.
Classic book for emotional healing from infant to adult. Textbook for seminars.

Bennett, Rita (1991). *Emotionally Free Course.* Edmonds, WA: CRA Publishing.
The Basic Course for small group or seminar presentation, 150 pgs., illustrations. For more information, see: www.EmotionallyFree.org.

Bennett, Rita (2005). *Holy Spirit and You Gifts Course.* Edmonds, WA: CRA Publishing.
Course or seminar presentation on nine supernatural gifts, 14 chapters, illustrations.

Bennett, Dennis and Rita (1971). *The Holy Spirit and You.* Alachua, FL: Bridge-Logos Publishing.
Classic book on Holy Spirit empowerment and the supernatural gifts—useful as a textbook.

Bennett, Dennis and Rita (2005). *The Holy Spirit and You Workbook.* Alachua, FL: Bridge-Logos Publishers.
For individual or small groups; it elaborates on the 18 chapters of the textbook.

Bennett, Rita, (2003). *Treasures from an Oak Chest.* Edmonds, WA: Healing People Publishing House.

Church, J.R. and Stearman, Gary (1993), *The Mystery of the Menorah*. Oklahoma City, OK: Prophecy Publications.

Fragrant Potpourri, Theological Treasures, Christmas and Hanukkah Lights, For Fun Limericks, Family Album, plus memoirs behind the scenes.

MacIlravy, Cora Harris (1916). *Christ And His Bride*. Chicago, IL: The Elbethel Christian Work.
An Exposition of the Song of Solomon.

Levitt, Zola (1979). *The Seven Feasts of Israel*. Dallas, TX: ZLM Online Store.
A complete explanation of the holy days God gave Moses on Mount Sinai, and how each was fulfilled by our Lord. Also includes explanations of their meanings for today.

Schlessinger, Dr. Laura (1998). *The Ten Commandments*. New York, NY: HarperCollins.
An impacting book on a much needed topic, written with Judeo-Christian understanding.

From Bridge-Logos

Books by Dennis and Rita Bennett

www.bridgelogos.com